Thomas Chalmers Murray

Lectures on the Origin and Growth of the Psalms

Thomas Chalmers Murray

Lectures on the Origin and Growth of the Psalms

ISBN/EAN: 9783337005412

Printed in Europe, USA, Canada, Australia, Japan

Cover: Foto ©ninafisch / pixelio.de

More available books at **www.hansebooks.com**

LECTURES

ON THE

ORIGIN AND GROWTH

OF THE

PSALMS

BY

THOMAS CHALMERS MURRAY

ASSOCIATE PROFESSOR OF THE SHEMITIC LANGUAGES AT THE
JOHNS HOPKINS UNIVERSITY.

NEW YORK
CHARLES SCRIBNER'S SONS
743 and 745 Broadway
1894

COPYRIGHT BY
CHARLES SCRIBNER'S SONS
1881

THIS VOLUME

IS

INSCRIBED

TO

DANIEL C. GILMAN,

PRESIDENT OF THE JOHNS HOPKINS UNIVERSITY,

AS ONE WHO WELCOMES THAT NEW ERA OF THOUGHT IN WHICH
ITS AUTHOR HAD HOPED TO BE A WORKER, AND
IN RECOGNITION OF PERSONAL AND
OFFICIAL RELATIONS.

PUBLISHERS' NOTE.

The following lectures were delivered at the Johns Hopkins University, during the winter of 1878-79, before a general audience. The form in which they were given was probably not that in which their author would have finally embodied his researches, or have permanently submitted them as a subject of scholarly criticism.

It has seemed, however, to many beside the publishers of this volume, that these lectures should be placed before a larger audience; not simply as the only completed work left by a scholar of very remarkable independence and promise, but as a most valuable contribution to the study to which his life was devoted—the reverent and critical investigation of the History and Literature of the Hebrew Scriptures. It is entirely certain that Professor Murray's early death, occurring but a few days after the closing of this course, took from his branch of learning one of the most earnest and able students it has counted in America.

Before the publication of these lectures, it was necessary to add to a few passages brief explanatory notes, verifications of references, transliterations, &c., such as the author himself would have supplied to aid the general reader unacquainted with Oriental languages. This scholarly service has been very kindly performed for the volume by the Rev. Dr. C. H. Toy, who has, however, in every case, affixed his initial to the note thus furnished.

CONTENTS.

LECTURE I.

ORIGIN AND HISTORY OF THE SHEMITIC PEOPLES. IMPORTANCE OF THE STUDY OF THEIR LANGUAGES AND LITERATURE, . . 1

LECTURE II.

HISTORY OF THE HEBREW LANGUAGE AND EARLY LITERATURE. COLLECTION OF THE HEBREW WRITINGS, ... 34

LECTURE III.

TITLES OF THE HEBREW SCRIPTURES. HISTORY OF THE NAMES PSALM AND PSALTER. LITERARY AND EDITORIAL ARRANGEMENT OF THE BOOKS OF THE PSALTER. INSCRIPTIONS OF THE PSALMS, ... 73

LECTURE IV.

THEORIES OF MACCABEAN AUTHORSHIP. ANTIOCHUS EPIPHANES AND THE MACCABEAN ERA. DAVIDIC AUTHORSHIP, . . . 110

LECTURE V.

ORIGIN AND METHOD OF COLLECTION OF THE DAVIDIC TEMPLE

BOOK. DAVID AS A POET, ... 144

LECTURE VI.

POST-EXILIC COLLECTORS. THE GREAT SYNAGOGUE. FIRST
AND SECOND BOOKS OF THE PSALTER. LYRICS OF THE SONS
OF KORAH, ... 175

LECTURE VII.

SECOND BOOK OF THE PSALTER. BALLAD POETRY. THE
ANONYMOUS PSALMS. THE VINDICTIVE PSALMS. NEHEMIAH.
THIRD BOOK OF THE PSALTER. LYRIC, EPIC AND DIDACTIC
POETRY. SONGS OF ASAPH, ... 209

LECTURE VIII.

DRAMATIC ART AMONG THE SHEMITES. TRAGEDY AND COMEDY
BOOK OF JOB. THE SONG OF SONGS. FOURTH BOOK OF
THE PSALTER, ... 247

LECTURE IX.

FIFTH BOOK OF THE PSALTER. THE SONGS OF DEGREES
COLLECTION OF THE FIVE BOOKS. SHEMITIC SONG AND
MUSIC. MUSICAL INSCRIPTIONS OF THE PSALMS. THE MUSIC
OF THE SECOND TEMPLE, ... 281

ORIGIN

AND

GROWTH OF THE PSALMS.

LECTURE I.

As the curtain rises on the stage of history, we can just descry through the mists of the early dawning, a Bedouin people dwelling in the Petræan uplands, between the Bight of Akaba and the Persian Gulf. They were the progenitors of perhaps the most unique and remarkable people whom the world has produced; a people belonging to a race and speech alien to our own, yet to whom we are under a greater obligation for our religion, our culture and our civilization, than to any of our own kin.

It was the beginnings of a people known to us under the unfortunate and misleading name, Shemitic, given them by Schlözer[1] at the close of the

[1] A. L. Schlözer in his article on the Chaldeans in Eichhorn's *Repertorium für biblische und morgenländische litteratur*, Part 8, p. 161

last century. [Semitic and Semite, now so much in vogue as almost to be good usage, are survivals of the French nomenclature of the English orientalists who learned Arabic at the feet of De Sacy.]

It seems appropriate at the opening of this course of lectures, among the first, if I mistake not, delivered in this country on the Shemitic Languages and Literature on the purely academic side and away from the restrictions inseparable from theological teaching, that I should glance briefly and in a way more popular than is possible in the class-room, at the position and history of this people, the exposition of one of whose literatures is our main object.

Of course the first question naturally arising in our minds is whence and how came this people to Arabia? but at the very threshold of this investigation we are met by problems as yet unsolved, for whose solution we scarce know where to look. The methods by which we trace them to Arabia are too technical for popular exposition; they are chiefly linguistic, though susceptible of as high a degree of

---

(1781) seems to speak of the term "Shemitic" as if he were its inventor, and its use in that article is the earliest, so far as appears. But Eichhorn himself in his *Allgemeine Bibliothek der biblischen litteratur*, vi. 772 (1794), claims to have been the first to substitute "Shemitic" for "Oriental" (the previous designation of these languages), and he must have known of Schlözer's use of it. It was through Eichhorn that the term gained currency. (T.)

proof as is possible outside the exact sciences—but here we suddenly lose the trail. Do we inquire of history, it is voiceless, for history had not yet begun. Do we interrogate their native traditions, we find them confused and contradictory, and in their earliest form bearing evidence of being loans from neighboring peoples rather than of native growth. Perchance you may bethink yourself of the Jewish records, and ask whether there be not in them some clue through the maze. These fragments of the infant history of the world, sacred in themselves and hallowed by association, no one who hears me can lay more stress on than myself. But what do they mean? What are those strange and majestic shapes thrown by the brush of the inspired artist athwart the background of his canvas? Do they represent persons, or peoples, or countries? Are they, as some claim, merely types, and if so, are these types ethnic or moral? Can we be sure that we have all the links in the chain, or has the writer chosen only those more prominent names which have projected themselves into the knowledge of his own time? This is not the place nor this a fit occasion to take up or answer these questions. They belong to the special problems which arise in discussing the Mosaic literature. I merely allude to them as questions not yet settled, on which there is a diversity well-

torians of civilization and dilettante biographers have so long held the public ear, that Arabic scholars should be heard on the character of Muhammed and the originality of his message. The Arab biographers but half conceal under their laudation of him as of purest lineage from the bluest blood of the desert, his descent from a mongrel tribe of traders—Qureish— formed through the mixture of Arabs, Jews, perhaps even Abyssinians, (the Abbasides had unmistakable negro blood) around the caravan stations at Mecca. The boy Muhammed learned from his uncle Waraka and the Jewish relatives of his mother the stories of their people. The prophet of Allah only reproduces them in the Koran, distorted by his diseased fancy, shaped to serve the ends of his ambition or appetite, and mingled with the fables of the people among whom he dwelt.

There is no pre-Islamite history or *native* tradition of the North Arabic people. The Bedouins make no history, and the native traditions of their origin have disappeared as irrecoverably as the tents of which one of their poets sings.—" Yesterday they gleamed white before me, but now are they vanished into desert air."

Even less can the accounts of the later Arab chroniclers lay claim to be used in serious history; they are merely the projection of the century immediately preceding Muhammed on a canvas they spanned to dimensions learned from other peoples. If the truth were known it would appear that we can not ascertain with surety even the names of the Prophet's ancestors at the second remove, so you may imagine the value of the genealogies of their eponymous heroes so liberally drawn on by the historians of the orient. Shemitic native traditions are like the prophetic reed on which scholars have only leaned to the piercing of their own hands.

Do we turn to philology for the solution of the problem of the origin of the Shemitic people, the reply is almost equally unsatisfactory. As I have had occasion tô say at a former time in this place, there are no Shemitic languages, but only one Shemitic language, whose various dialects differ from one another hardly as much as do the dialects of the Greek. After eliminating some few differences of vocabulary accidental to the kinds of literature in which the one or the other dialect has come down to us, the difference between the most widely variant of them would be about the same as exists in our own day between the German of the Hanoverian heaths and that of the Bavarian highland, or, if you please, between the English of the midland and the border counties. Of these dialects the Arabic is the most interesting, as it is most copious and most characteristically Shemitic. The Hebrew, which is more commonly studied and taken as the type of the language, is, in the form in which it has been preserved to us, philologically the latest and least characteristic. When we come to sift and compare these dialects, we find them all unmistakably pointing to the old Arabic as their earliest form, to the Steppes of the Nejd [1] as their primeval home. But there they stop, and in vain do we seek in them a clue to lead us further.

The comparisons drawn and made so much of by those holding briefs for the primitive unity of speech, between the Shemitic and our own family of language are in the main delusive, being founded on mere accordances of sound in decayed forms of one family or the other—between the Latin and the Hebrew for example, where this species of philology has most run riot. Of grammatical resemblance, the only infallible test of relationship in language, there is no trace, as there seems a well-nigh insuperable barrier between the original Indo-European with its mobile vowels and the stiff vowelless Shemitic.

The evidence on one side or the other is simply not in a condition for the cautious philologist to make use of. No doubt in the end, the problem of the primitive unity of the Shemitic and Indo-European may shape itself differently, but we must bear in mind

[1] The Arabian highland stretching toward Babylonia. (T.)

that for the present the trend of the evidence is to prove a radical diversity, and many of the most conservative Shemitic philologists, as Nöldeke, deny the possibility of any unity of origin for speeches so inherently dissimilar. However the result may be, the evidence of language to those who have no interest save philology at stake, does *not now* point to any common home, where as has been fondly believed Shemite and Aryan dwelt together, does *not* enable us to trace Shemitic speech back to some more primitive form. If we glance over the peoples who lay around the Shemites as they appear in history, it will but further show them to us as a racial oasis in their deserts, a waif in the midst of alien peoples. Immediately on the north in the Babylonian lowlands and at the river mouths was a *Turanian* [1] people akin to the European Magyars and Fins; further northward along the upper river courses lay a people whose name and very existence was unknown to us

[1] The term "Turanian" (formed from *Tur*, the name of a mythical personage in the Persian legends) was invented by Max Müller, and is used by him and others to include all languages except those of the Indo-European, Shemitic and Hamitic (this term embracing sub-Shemitic, Egyptian and Libyan) families—that is, almost all the agglutinizing and monosyllabic languages of the world. Others confine it to the agglutinizing groups: Ugro-Finnish, Samoyed, Turco-Tatar and Tongous, and still others reject it altogether as meaningless and misleading. In fact it does not in itself convey either a geographical or a linguistic meaning, and is open to the same objections as the name "Shemitic." Probably the author here uses it in the second of the above senses, in which the Accadian also would be included. (T.)

until within a few years, their antiquities have been unearthed from the mounds of Karkhemish.[1] The Mediterranean sea-board was held by tribes to whom the imagination of the later Shemitic inhabitants has given Titanic proportions, the Anakim and Zamzummim—the African coast was held by a Hottentot people, at a later time pushed southward by the successive waves of immigration.

Do we call anthropology to our aid with its measurements of the skull and minute investigation of the crinkle of the hair and color of the skin, we shall find the diversity between the Shemites and their neighbors even far more deeply seated than the variance of their customs, their civilizations and their religions had *a priori* led us to assume.

Thus we may say with accuracy and without flinching any of the points at issue, that the beginning of Shemitic history is concident with the appearance of the Shemitic people in Arabia. Further than this we cannot venture safely with the clues now in our hands. I do not however wish to be understood as holding with Sprenger and the later Shemitic ethnologists that the Shemites are the autochthonous

[1] Inscriptions in an unknown character have been found at Hamath, Karkhemish and in Asia Minor. The character is usually called Hamathite, and has as yet defied decipherment; almost absolutely nothing is known of the people and language to which it belonged. See the publications of the London Society of Biblical Archæology. (T.)

Bedouin race of Arabia, a theory assuming the whole point at issue. My philological instinct leads me to believe that there are some few ground principles common to all speech, which careful investigation will one day discover and establish. It is for the Shemitic philologist to help on the solution by sifting out in the mass of phenomena with which he has to deal the merely accidental, from that which is essential and permanent. I also believe there is a discoverable (though not yet discovered) bond of union between the Shemitic and the other peoples. It is the part of the student of Shemitic civilization to distinguish what is characteristic in their racial features and habits of mind from what is merely the outgrowth of their environment.

The first step in every science is to stake out the boundaries between the known and the unknown, and there would be no stimulus to further work, if philology or ethnology unlocked their secrets, save to the most patient research.

Looking out now from this vantage-ground we have gained in Arabia, let me ask you to follow me as I cursorily sketch the way in which the hither Orient became settled by the Shemites. It seems remarkable that the barren steppes of Tartary and Arabia, so alike in climate and in natural feature, should have been the *officinæ* of the two great peoples of the world. We are as yet unable to trace the reason for the strange seething and upheavals in Central Asia, whose resultant was the outpouring over Europe at longer or shorter intervals of the successive waves of Aryan immigration. It is in precisely a similar and equally mysterious way that the Western Orient has been Shemitized from Arabia.

The most remarkable of these Shemitic movements is one which has occurred within comparatively a few centuries and to which before the close of this lecture I shall have occasion to allude.

The most interesting question at the present in Shemitic philology is the relation between the Shemitic and a group of dialects which some one in a luckless hour dubbed Hamitic. By Hamitic is meant the Old Egyptian and its outgrowth the vulgar dialects of the Coptic; further the dialects of the peoples who since the earliest times have lain along the edge of the Sahara from Syrtis to the Atlas, just back of the fringe of various civilizations, Carthaginian, Latin and Arabic, which had successively held the Mediterranean seaboard of Africa. These dialects may without hesitation be placed under one head and regarded as a single group. When we come to compare them with the Shemitic we are at once struck with so many apparent resemblances, lying as it were on their very surface, that we are fain to regard them as Shemitic dialects. When we further investigate their nominal and verbal formation we find such deep-seated diversity as to force us to an entire remodeling of our theories of Shemitic structure, should they be admitted as well-authenticated members of this group. I think you cannot fail to see how radical will be the reshaping of history if Egyptian letters and civilization be proven to be outgrowths of the Shemitic stock. But we must turn away from the too tempting vista; the question still sways in air. Shemitic scholarship, to its shame be it said, has left this problem of such supreme importance unwrought, for discussions as to technical minutiæ of the Jewish schoolmen, which it is a wonder can be of interest to any occidental mind. If the result show a connection between the Shemitic and the so called Hamitic, the Hamitic must be regarded as the earliest surge of the Shemitic migrations passing away from the parental home, before there had become fixed and crystalized in the Shemitic those linguistic features so characteristic of it at a later day, and acquiring from the tribes they found in the Nile valley those Nigritian features which have led many to assign the Egyptian to the African dialects. In other words, the Hamitic will only be a species of *Pre-Shemitic*.[1]

---

[1] More exactly: one branch of the primitive Hamitic-Shemitic stem, the other branch being the Shemitic. (T.)

Leaving this for future inquiry and turning now to the migrations of the people recognized as Shemitic, we see first the invasion of the Euphrates valley at a period not prior to the year 3000 before our era. We have now-a-days too many Oriental chronologies to set much confidence in any of them; the eloquent satire of Macaulay on Hindu chronology in his Memoranda on Indian Education, would be apropos to the Berosian dynasties with their thousands and ten thousands of years. We can easily understand how the rich reaches of river bottom, which until this day make Babylonia one of the gardens of the Lord, early attracted the Arab Bedouin across the narrow rim of desert which was their only protection; how the commerce of the Indies in its earliest trade line up the Persian Gulf tempted, as it has done almost five thousand years later, Arab pirates to lurk along the shores and infest the river mouths. We must not conceive of any sudden conquest of the Accadian inhabitants; year by year the Bedouin raided deeper into the land—year by year the pirate fleets pressed further up the rivers until they became strong enough to seize the reins of government. On the earliest inscriptions the Shemitic element is but the ruling caste among a people Turanian in speech, in manners and in religion.[1] The welding together of the two

[1] The Accadians and the Sumerians, who were probably two tribes of

peoples came slowly, and at a later period seems far from perfect—in fact there are doubts whether the population of Babylonia ever became homogeneous. In this process the Shemitic element lost well-nigh all save their language; they acquired from their more cultured subjects their civilization and religion. So it comes to pass that when the North Shemites begin to emigrate from Babylonia, which had become a new centre for them, they carry away with their Shemitic speech Turanian mythology, Turanian civilization and Turanian manners. Therefore it is, I have said at the beginning of this lecture, that much of the Shemitic tradition is not of native growth. We find among the Arab Bedouin of the present day, who have remained in the old homes, customs and beliefs more characteristically Shemitic than those disclosed to us by the very earliest of the North Shemitic monuments.

Long ere the Shemitic invaders had gained the mastery in Babylonia the more hardy spirits began pushing up the river valleys, and joined doubtless by nomad bands who had come through the desert, they dispossessed the feeble upland folk and laid the foundations of the Aramaic people.

the same people, and have probably left traces of themselves in a good many of the proper names of that region, among others, in the names Tigris, Euphrates and Ur (Abraham's city). See Lenormant's *La langue primitive de la Chaldée.* (T.)

The peculiarities of Aramaic speech have been the peg on which the school who endeavor to trace a Shemitic dispersion from Central Asia have hung their beliefs. Their theory is that in the Shemitic dispersions the Arameans were a waif who tarried behind in the hill country while the main body pushed forward into Arabia. The testimony of language will however, I think, disprove convincingly any such origin of the Aramaic people; if it be of any value, it shows that the Aramaic possesses, in common with the older Shemitic, forms which can only be explained by a prolonged sojourn in Arabia, and a later attrition by coming into contact with the Turanian people in Babylonia.

The Arameans were traders and adventurers; the mart they founded at Nineveh first rivalled and then surpassed the capital of their older brethren further down the rivers, while the wars of a later day between Assyria and Babylon were an internecine struggle for the control of the trade lines. As the India trade passed gradually to the Himyarite settlements on the south coast of Arabia, the Euphrates valley lost its wealth, its power and its prestige, and fell a prey to the Aryan hordes who had been long hovering along its Eastern frontier. Never must we forget the debt of obligation which civilization owes to the Arameans; pressing into Asia Minor through their mountain defiles they early seized the coasts and islands of the Egean. It is possible they were in Greece before the Hellens reached there. It is they and not the Phenicians who are the fabled Cadmus (*Qadma*, Eastern people) who brought us our letters. It was they whose science, crude as it was, kindled the torch which in the hands of the Greeks was to blaze into a flame; from their rude art it was that the Greeks learned the elements of their magnificent architecture.[1] Within our own era they have done a work for civilization the credit of which has been given to others, scarcely less precious than that of the early time. When the Greek learning fled from the ecclesiastical strife and civil disorder of the lower empire, it largely took refuge in the Aramaic university of Edessa, than where the Aristotelian philosophy has

---

[1] It is necessary to distinguish carefully between the Arameans and the Assyrians, two peoples dwelling side by side in the Tigris-Euphrates valley, yet quite distinct in language, character and achievements. It was the Assyrians that founded Nineveh, and became the teachers of the Greeks in architecture (as may reasonably be inferred from the similarity between the architectural remains found at Mycenæ and Nineveh). It may be that the Greek letters were derived from the Arameans, and that they early penetrated to the western sea; but this early history is obscure, and we shall have to wait for the results of further investigation and discovery before forming an opinion on the relations between the East and the West in the pre-historic time. Compare the author's remarks p. 14. (T.)

been nowhere cherished by more loving hands. Syrian scholars were the masters of the untrained Arabs of the armies of Islam, and it is merely what they learned from them that the Arabs carried to Spain, to kindle there the new learning and to open the Renascence. Dr. Draper gives to the torchbearer the credit which belongs to the flame. The native Arabs have neither a creative nor a scientific mind. Count the great names who in the middle ages made Arabic science illustrious, and you will find that almost without exception, in the orient they are Arameans or Persians—in the occident Spanish Jews or Moors.

But we must pass from the Arameans with a single word further. They held the upper courses of the Euphrates and Tigris until they were obliterated by new incursions from Arabia in the sixth century of our era. Their dialect was with its slight inflections the English of the Shemitic family: as the tradespeech of the orient it had by the second century before our era, displaced all the kindred North Shemitic dialects. It is of interest as being in its Galilean patois the mother tongue of Christ and his first followers—the speech in which thought the men who wrote the New Testament in Greek. It is preserved to us carved on the Palmyrene monuments, hewn in the Petrean rocks, treasured in a voluminous literature, still spoken in half a dozen corrupt jargons through the Lebanon and in Persia.

At a time no doubt somewhat later, as the river valleys became overcrowded, there pushed out into the lowland the first spur of the Canaanite people who took possession of the Mediterranean seaboard, and are known to us by the name given them in the occident, Phenicians. They were the traders of the early times, whose colonies formed a *Hansabund* across the then known world, from the shores of the Euxine to the tin mines of Cornwall. The Carthage, "the new city," founded by them to command the African trade, has to most of us, from school days, been the chief representative of their greatness. The study of their mythology and art on which so much stress is laid in these days, will prove of small value, as both were borrowed by them from the Assyrians; but the investigation of their political institutions and commercial code is of value even in America, which has not advanced so greatly beyond them.

It is an apothegm come of late into most histories of the world, that the Shemitic peoples were not traders or colonists. Ground is gained for this hypothesis by excluding from the Shemitic peoples the Phenicians. The only reason for this exclusion is a faulty interpretation of certain genealogies of the Genesis, but the Phenicians cannot be kept out; they are too plainly marked as of the Shemitic type to be excluded by any ex-cathedra judgment. Even if they were excluded, it is hard to see what vantage the holders of this view would gain, with the colonies and trade of so clearly Shemitic peoples as the Arameans and Himyarites still unaccounted for.

The second Shemitic migration into the lowland was that of the Palestinian tribes, of whom hardly more is preserved to us than their names and some few words in the Hebrew writings.

The third and last was that of the Terahites, who entered the lowland about 2000 B.C., long after it was settled by the kindred tribes who had preceded them. The great mass of these settled down in Canaan; only a small fragment, attracted by the inducements held out by the Hyksos, pass on, at a later day, into the pasture land of the Eastern Nile Delta. With their expulsion begins the more specific Israelite history, which I will take up briefly when I speak of their literature in the next hour. Bear in mind one thing rarely noted, that the name Hebrew (*Ibri*, of which, by the way, we have no satisfactory solution) belongs in common to all the Terahite people ; there is no reason for applying it to the Israelites any more than to the Edomites or Ishmaelite Arabs. Good English usage ·goes for something even in nomenclature, and so we continue to say Hebrew, Hebrew people, and Hebrew writings. But if we wish to be exact we must say Israel. Hebrew is, as I have said, the name of the whole Abrahamic people; Jew but a name of a single Israelite tribe.

During the thousand or fifteen hundred years through which the North Shemitic countries were being settled, there was taking place a similar, though far less important movement, to the southward. At a period somewhat subsequent to the Shemitic settlement of the Euphrates valley, Arab settlers reached the shores of the Indian Ocean and became the nucleus of the Himyarite people. Like their brethren, the Phenicians, they were adventurous traders and mariners, and at an early day succeeded in diverting the Indian trade from the Persian Gulf.. Their little skiffs, following the favorable turn of the Monsoon, carried rapidly and safely the spices and ivories of India from the Malabar coast to their own ports, whence they were conveyed by caravan to Egypt and the Phenician distributing depots for the occident. The huge and shapeless ruins which are found throughout Yemen attest their being a wealthy and magnificent people. The Greeks, misinterpreting their name Himyar, called the sea on which they lived and traded 'Ερυθρή, "The Red." [1]

[1] Himyar, the pretended eponym of the Himyarites, is a legendary person who, an uncertain number of centuries before the beginning of

At a comparatively late time, probably not many centuries before our era, there was an emigration of Himyarites across the Bab-el-Mandab, بَابُ الـمَانلَبَ ("Gate of Tears," Gate of Sighs, leading into the dangerous, narrow sea, feared till the present day by mariners,) into Africa. Their name, Geez, "The Free," leads us to suppose they may have been political refugees from Himyarite authority, which we know was none of the mildest. Christianized, but little improved, in the fourth century by Greek missionaries, they have become known to the occident as Ethiopic. Of late there has been much interest shown for them in connection with the English Expedition against Theodore. Their dialect is linguistically of great importance for Shemitic phonology, but their meagre literature of homilies and translations is devoid of interest.

Beyond the Ethiopic, probably stretching to the south of the Equator, were a number of negro dialects partly Shemitized through contact with the Ethiopians, known as *Sub-Shemitic*. These dialects have been first brought to notice by English and German explorers or missionaries during the present

our era, is said to have raised his tribe to pre-eminence among the Sabean people, and to have founded the famous and powerful Himyaritic kingdom, which continued till its overthrow by the Abyssinians in the sixth century after Christ. The name is somewhat similar in form and sound to an Arabic word meaning "red." (T.)

century, so their extent and peculiarities are as yet imperfectly understood.

Thus we have glanced over the migrations of the Shemitic peoples up to the beginning of our era. A view of the map will show the territory occupied by them as a somewhat irregular parallelogram between the Indian Ocean on the south, the Persian Gulf and the Tigris on the east, the Taurus on the north, and the Mediterranean and the Red Sea on the west. You will observe that Arabia covers at least two-thirds of this. Beyond these limits the Shemitic people save in the case of the feeble rim of refugees across the Bab-el-Mandab, do not seem to have spread save sporadically; the Phenician colonies were no more than trading posts, and the Arameans were early pressed back out of their settlements on the Egean. This peculiarly Shemitic territory is no larger than European Russia—a narrow stage on which have been enacted some of the grandest scenes of the world's drama.

No sketch however, of the Shemitic nation, can be complete without noticing the most far-reaching of their migrations, that strange movement within our own era, by which the oldest of their peoples sud-' denly burst, sword in hand, from their deserts, to change the faith and the culture of half the civilized world. The beginnings of this movement can be traced back to a period shortly after the opening of our era, when the change of trade-lines reduced the resources of the people of Yemen. The Ghassanites and Tayites,[1] severally the frontier people of the Roman and Persian power, who had to bear the brunt of every attack, were South Arabic peoples who first reached the Syrian frontiers in the third century of our era. The movement continued with gathering volume during the next two centuries. Shortly before Muhammed, a Himyarite tribe had with difficulty been expelled from Mecca. It was as a sort of neutral umpire, between two warring clans of the South, who had seized Medina, that the prophet was called thither. It is a mistake to suppose that the Arab conquest was due primarily, either to Muhammed or to Islam. He was a child of fortune, whose faith, believed in and often taught before him, unheeded, by men of greater genius and purer character than his own, was proclaimed just as the time had grown ripe, and became a rallying cry through which the Bedouin, hitherto possessing no common centre, were united. Mayhap he hastened the bursting of the storm, but even without him the storm would soon have broken. I wish to impress on your mind that the movements which led to the re-peopling of the Orient in the sixth

---

[1] The Ghassanites dwelt at Bosra in Syria, and the Tayites near the mountains Aja and Salma. (T.)

century of our era, were primarily national, precisely the same in kind with those which long ages before, had given it its first Shemitic population. Omar, Abu-Bakr and the shrewder minds who controlled the Prophet, succeeded in turning his somewhat variegated revelations to good account. The sudden military success of the Bedouin need not surprise us; the Roman Empire had long out-lived its day; rent by dissensions, and rotten with corruption, it was shivered by the first impact of the fresh blood of the desert. Within scarce fifty years from the death of the Orthodox Caliphs, the Arabs had conquered almost all the countries of the Mediterranean, which it had taken the Latin legionaries and administrators centuries to subdue and order. As little need the success of Islam be a surprise; the Orient had grown weary of being harried by the strifes of warring sectaries, and torn asunder by discordant ecclesiastics who had almost forgotten there was a God in their endless discussions as to His nature and persons— the Greek dialectics of Alexandria and Byzantium, confused minds susceptible only of a tangible and simple creed. So it was that a large part of the Orient was ready without compulsion and without persecution to accept the simpler confession and ritual of Islam. That the Arabs were persecutors cannot be doubted, but their faith would never have been so successful had there not been a preparedness for it in the people they subdued. I hope, if occasion offer, at some future time to speak of the rise of the Saracen power; we cannot now pause to speak of it. Unused to rule any save the simple children of the desert, untrained in the arts of government, their hands were too feeble to grasp the sceptre of the world's empire, which had fallen to them. The dynasties of the Omeyades and Abbasides furnish a black succession of voluptuaries and tyrants, hardly redeemed by the genius of a Maimun or the piety of an Omar II. The pretorian band of Turkish mercenaries first called in by the Caliphs to protect them from the indignation of their oppressed and outraged subjects, speedily became strong enough to seize the califate to themselves, and after four thousand years the control of the Orient passed back into the hands of the Turanians who held it at the very dawn of its history. The Arab language, however, maintained itself, and has been an ever increasing power in the East. It is one of the most graceful and forcible of civilized tongues—the mother tongue of millions of people, and commonly spoken from the pillars of Hercules to the wall of China, from the shores of the Caspian to the equator. Travelers tell us that both on the North and South, it is still spreading. It has a literature more considerable than that of any occidental nation, covering all branches of human thought and endeavor, in itself of great value and interest to western scholars. There has been scarcely a time in the history of the Shemitic dialects when they could so ill as now be classed under "ancient languages and literature."

After this imperfect and hasty sketch of the Shemitic people, let me in conclusion say a word as to the proper position of the study of the Shemitic languages in an University course of instruction.

Of chief importance is this study from the standpoint of Philology. No philology worthy of the name is exhausted by the study and teaching of a single language, or family of languages. Philology is an investigation into the phenomena of all articulate thought. As the geologist traces through his rock strata the growth of the earth, as the biologist follows through his orders the development of life, so it is the task of the philologist to trace through the various languages of the world, the origin and development of that most characteristic, yet most recondite faculty of the human race—speech. One cannot wonder that of late years what is called comparative philology has been in growing disrepute. Even as pursued by the wiser scholars it has been founded almost entirely upon the observation of the phenomena of our own family, and so has broken down or proved inadequate, when brought face to face with the larger phenomena of speech. The old adage of "one language—no language," is being verified as to many of its hasty generalizations which are proving too narrow even for Indo-Germanic structure. Of course in our day it would be folly for any philologist to take all language as his province, or even to hope to master a single family. It is only by most patient painstaking investigation and analysis of the different dialects by many different scholars, that we can ever hope to reach the ultimate facts upon which may be built up a synthesis of enduring value and truth for all speech.

Next of kin to our own family stands the Shemitic as the second great language of the civilized peoples; its structure, composed solely of consonantal elements, marvelously compact and singularly unique, has on the surface apparently no analogy in our own family. The first problem for serious philology to decide is the relation between these two families. It is to be the crucial test of the value of philological methods. If they are unequal to solving and settling the relations of languages so contiguous, contemporaneous through well nigh six thousand years, and easily accessible in a voluminous literature, we may well despair of any success with the outlying and obscurer families. This investigation involves as well questions of even more far-reaching importance. If in the several analyses of the Shemitic and Indo-European it be found that their ultimate elements and methods are so inherently dissimilar as to preclude not only the development of one from the other, but even from a common stock, it will create an argument against an original unity of human speech, and hence *a priori* against an original unity of the human race. If the present apparent diversity be proved superficial on investigation, there will doubtless be disclosed early methods of formation enabling us more clearly to see the principle of human speech underlying the now utterly discordant mass of spoken language. No larger investigation, however, can be of value without an accurate, and, as far as may be, exhaustive acquaintance with the several languages at issue.

In scarce any field are there more problems lying unwrought whose working promises so rich results. The language of the mighty empires of the Euphrates, unearthed during this century, from the mounds of Nineveh, stands patiently waiting under the indignities it suffers at prentice hand of tyros, for some scholar to bring a master key to its arcana. What people carved the inscriptions of Petra? What is the clue through the Hamathite characters? What the interpretation of the Himyarite monuments? What is the origin of the written character become ours by later inheritance from the Shemite? These are but a tithe of the opening problems in which one need tread no hackneyed round, but may strike out for himself in unknown fields as a discoverer. Or come to the trodden ground of the better known dialects, none of which, not even the Hebrew, studied one is oft fain to say these eighteen hundred years to small purpose, has been thoroughly investigated. He will be doing original work, deserving well of philology, who collects all the phenomena of even the smallest of them in a scientific grammar or glossary.

But philological investigation can not proceed far without the aid of the literary instinct; it goes halting through an arid waste of logomachy unless there be in the literatures studied inherent value and interest. Shemitic literature is of interest to the occidental student, and in what I have to say of it I exclude the Israelitish writings, which I shall speak of in a subsequent hour.

First of all, as pure *literature*. Its style (so essentially different from that of most Aryan peoples), should be of interest to us, as our language, under the influence of the English Bible, has, to a degree of which many are unconscious, been Shemitized. The poetry of the Bedouin, sprung from their transparent air and long reaches of desert, lacks, perhaps, that perfect form and workmanship in which the Greeks are masters of the world. But in what lies nearer to the essence of true poetry, the power to paint nature and gather in a single word the manifold expression of earth and sky, it is approached by no other literature. But the very analytic character of the Shemitic mind which gives such beauty to the minute pictures of their poetry, is a disadvantage to their prose style. This is broad, and loses in its mass of detail the synthetic brevity and clearness of statement which, to the better taste of the Aryans, is essential to good style. If read at all with interest it must be for ends other than literary, and chief of these is the *historical.* It is but little understood how much of history, and to us most interesting history, is contained solely in Shemitic literature. The traditions of the beginning of the Turanian people, and the history of the powers who ruled the civilized world from the twentieth to the eighth century before our era is stamped on the Assyrian tablets; the commencements of the world's trade and commerce are carved on the Phenician and Himyarite stones; or leaving the dead past and coming to movements within our own era, where shall we look but to the annals of the Syriac chroniclers for the history of the last great incursion of the barbarian hordes in which the curse of God, Kenghiz Khan, ravaged the fairest portions of earth and swept away with his besom of fire and blood the last traces of antique civilization? Where shall we look, one might almost say, for the history of the world during the night of mediæval superstition and barbarism, when Europe scarce had a history, but to the scholars of Bagdad and Cordova? The very faults of Shemitic style make their documents of the greatest historical value —we have an almost painfully detailed rehearsal of the minutiæ of the facts known to their compiler— rarely redeemed, the historian might say marred, by being fused through his conception of them into a synthetic whole.

The history of civilization is also largely beholden to the student of Shemitic manners and beliefs.

Renan in his history, graceful as fiction and scarce more trustworthy, has evolved a theory of the Shemitic monotheistic instinct which has almost become an integral part of every history of culture. But later investigation shows that hardly any people are of nature and intent so little monotheistic as the Shemites. The primitive Bedouin Shemite is a fetich-worshipper—he never advances into civilization in the early time save to become polytheistic. What is called the monotheistic instinct is clearly due to some impulse from without on a single branch of the Shemitic stock. It is no less one of the most interesting than one of the most important tasks of the student of civilization to trace this back to its fountain-head, follow it through the history of that mysterious fragment of our race whom it raised to a position of permanent influence and interest such as even Greek art and literature has failed to do for the Hellens, until it blossoms out into the two great religions of the world, Christianity and Islam. The religion of the western world, be it Judaism or Christianity, is stated in Shemitic terms; was first taught by a Shemitic tongue to a Shemitic people. The origin and primitive form of Christianity is inexplicable without understanding that the manners and habits of thought of its founders were Shemitic. The Greek element which later came into it and is so often confounded with it became an element of alienation to its Shemitic followers.

Turn in another direction and how valuable are the inquiries as to the genesis of the Assyrian art and letters, by contact with which in Asia Minor and the islands of the Egean our own art had its beginnings. Looking to the eastward, what is the relation between the early culture of India and the Euphrates valley, so like, yet so unlike? Looking to the westward, what precisely is the Shemitic element in the primitive Greek culture, what the Shemitic influence which has left traces so unmistakable in the rude art which has been exhumed in our day from Mycenæ and Hissarlik?

Only time fails me further to dwell on the many points of interest and importance in Shemitic study. I trust that this University which already in its beginnings has done so much for the elevation of American scholarship may be permitted to solve some of these problems. I trust Shemitic letters may never be regarded here as survivals of a scholastic learning whose usefulness has long since volatilized, may never be taught here to prove any dogma save truth. I trust they may be esteemed as of equal value with their sister branches of philology and literature for the study of the thought, the civilization and the history of the world.

I shall in continuation of this course of lectures take up, in our next hour, first a short sketch of the rise and development of the literature of the Jewish people, passing then to speak, more specially of the book of Psalms; the collection, arrangement and the present form of the entire book, together with the style, authorship and age of the several poems. This course is *not* designed for Hebrew scholars, so use will be made of the version of King James now in general acceptance in most English-speaking communities.

LECTURE II.

I ENDEAVORED in a previous hour to make clear to you the origin of the Shemitic peoples, and traced, after a cursory manner, the migrations by which they became masters of the hither Orient. I further endeavored to show the importance of the study of Shemitic letters and history to a just appreciation of the thought and civilization, not only of antiquity but even of our own time. Many of the points which I then merely touched might be further dwelt on with both interest and advantage. We must however turn now to the consideration of the language and literature of one of the smallest and politically least important of these Shemitic peoples—the Israelites.

The Hebrew literature is one of the cultured literatures of the world; as *literature* it suffers with most of us, through being removed by certain subjective standards from comparison with all other literatures. In what I have to say in this and the succeeding lectures, I shall regard it alone from the linguistic and literary side, which I trust will not be without interest in opening up some views which may prove novel to you. Believe me that I do so not from any unmindfulness of the sacred relations other than literary in which the Hebrew Scriptures must ever stand to us.

Take up any history of the Orient of a century ago and you will find stated as an axiom, to doubt which was well-nigh doubting an essential of faith, that the Hebrew was the mother-tongue of the race spoken in Eden by our first parents; for, naively says an old chronicler, "the divine name as well as that of the first human pair are plainly of the Hebrew tongue,"— the only fly in the pot of ointment being that the serpent seemed so conversant with this same divine language.

With the growing knowledge of the Orient and the renascence of philological study due to the discovery of the Sanscrit, it became apparent that any such origin of human speech was impossible; the miracles in language by which the Greek and Latin were derived in the olden time from the Hebrew are now for scholars but curiosities, of interest alone to the historian of philology. I have been surprised to find that even at the present day this view of the priority of the Hebrew retains such hold in the popular beliefs; but even going no further than the Hebrew Scripture, on ground of which the view is still held by some, it is capable of convincing disproof; for (1) the proper names which came down in the Mosaic writings from the antediluvian period are not Shemitic nor can they be explained from any Shemitic language, least of all from the Hebrew. The people to whom they belonged seem to have been members of an older non-Shemitic civilization, who held the orient before the rise of the Shemitic peoples. Scholars are in doubt as to who this earlier people were, though it seems the growing belief that they were akin to the present Turanians. However this may be, it is (2) clearly stated in the Genesis that the Terahite or Hebrew migration had its origin in the district of Ur, on the lower Euphrates. Almost contemporaneous slabs and tablets, of late years unearthed at Mugheir, show that the language spoken in Ur at the time of the Abrahamic migration must have been the Babylonian, thus strikingly confirming our assumption made on purely philological grounds in the last hour, that the Hebrew was developed through the Babylonian from some earlier Shemitic mother-tongue; and we find in Genesis xxxi. 47, that an older branch of the patriarchal families than that to which Abraham belonged lived in Mesopotamia and spoke not the Hebrew but the Aramaic.

Not to confuse or weary you with technical minutiæ, I will sum up the judgment of modern scholarship in a word by saying that what is known to us as *Hebrew* is the Shemitic dialect of the Palestinian seaboard of the Mediterranean, spoken with slight shades of variance, chiefly in vocabulary, by all the Palestinian peoples. Do you ask for proof of this, you may read it in clearest character in the broken fragments of the Mesha Stone,[1] oldest monument of the Palestinian people; on the ruins of the Phenician colonies, strewn on every coast of the Mediterranean, and in the names of the towns and peoples of the Canaanites, preserved to us in the writings of the nation who had dispossessed them.

The barriers which grew up in a later time were national and religious; linguistically there were none. Phenician, Philistine, Canaanite, and Israelite, all spoke patois of the same sea-coast dialect, probably in no case with such variance as would prevent perfect mutual understanding of one another. How this dialect, with its peculiar variations from the mother

[1] The Mesha stone or Moabite stone is a heavy basaltic block discovered in the year 1868 on the eastern side of the Dead Sea. It contains an inscription in the Moabitish dialect by the Moabite king Mesha, narrating the victories that his god Chemosh had given him over the Israelites; the inscription, belonging to the ninth century B. C., is a valuable contribution to Shemitic palæography, shows the close similarity of the Moabite and Israelite dialects, and throws light on the history of the Omri dynasty. (T.)

tongue and the sister dialects, grew up, we can not as yet clearly see; it is, however, considered proven by the best Shemitic scholars that it grew up in Palestine from the meeting and attrition there of the various Shemitic invasions—Babylonian, Aramaic, and Arabic —during a longer or shorter period subsequent to the year 3000 before our era.

The migration who enter Palestine under Abraham, including not only the subsequent Israel but as well the Moabites, Edomites, Ammonites, and even the Ishmaelite Bedouin, who later held the northern edge of the Arabic desert, have the generic designation Hebrew (עִבְרִי *Ibri*), a little understood name, referring, perhaps, to their having come from beyond (עֵבֶר) the Euphrates—it is a name precisely of a sort with Canaan, (כְּנַעַן *Kenaan*), the national epithet of the previous immigration.

There is a mooted question which need not concern us here, as to whether the Abrahamic immigrants came in among the previous settlers speaking a language precisely similar to them, or whether they acquired their later dialect from the Canaanites. It is at all events clear from the narrative of the Genesis that the patriarchs settled on friendly terms among a people with whom they seem to have readily been able to communicate. The migration of a portion of the Abrahamites to Egypt, whither they had been attracted by the fertile lands of the Goshen delta and the largess of the Arab shepherd (Hyksos) dynasty, who had seized the reins of power, probably would do little to change their dialect, save in the vocabulary for things specifically Egyptian. The Egyptians were the most exclusive people of antiquity, regarding contact with the foreigner as pollution ; after the national movement which resulted in driving out the hated rule of the Hyksos, their Shemitic subjects were interned in slave colonies in the extreme part of the eastern boundaries. Breaking away from this bondage, it was the majestic revelation received through Moses which first united "the mixed multitude" into the people Israel, and gave to it that peculiar sense of nationality—a people dwelling alone—which so distinguishes them in the later history from their neighbor peoples, kindred in language and descent. Ibn Khaldun, the Hallam of Arab historians, in his "History of the Berbers," after describing in an eloquent passage the effect of the desert on the so-called civilized man of the town, in conclusion wisely and pithily suggests that there was need, throughout a generation, of the pure air and simple life of the desert to fit the vitiated and debased fugitives of Egypt to become a nation and the bearers of a revelation.[1] But however much revelation or surrounding may have shaped the

---

[1] This passage occurs in the Prolegomena to the History. (T.)

character of the people, there is no reason to believe their language underwent any change ; they lived and wandered among the Ishmaelite Arabs, who were an offspring of the same stock as themselves. There was no need for a linguistic conquest of Palestine. Though they came back a nation where they had gone forth a fragment, they bring back with them a language in all respects similar to the one they had taken away from their old home. With all the stress laid in scripture on the religious and national diversity between Israel and the Canaanites, never is there an allusion to so telling a point as linguistic difference might have made had it been present. The very name Israel gives their language, "the tongue of Canaan" (Isa. xix. 18, שְׂפַת כְּנַעַן), seems to imply what from other sources we know positively, that it was the common speech of all the dwellers of Canaan. The whole tone of the narratives in the Jewish historical books creates the impression that the people of Israel had easy and constant communication, without need of interpreter, with all their neighbors.

But while in the slavery of Egypt and the discipline of the desert, the Israelite people had been growing into a nation, there had unnoticed been encroaching on the northern frontier of Palestine a language which was destined to swallow up the old speech of Canaan. It was the Aramaic coming from

Mesopotamia and the upper Euphrates, to whose later growth as well as the reason of it I alluded in the last hour. The northern tribes of Israel, who barely conquered and never held their own, were at once thrown against this Aramaic frontier and very early begin to show signs of its influence. The song of Deborah, a war ballad composed and sung in the north, has forms which are unmistakably the result of this Aramaizing. Had not the rise of the Jewish kingdom under David and the increase of its wealth and power by the venturesome but successful commercial policy of Solomon furnished a centre for the national life, Israel would, long ere it did, have succumbed to the pressure from the north. Moreover the establishment of the Temple in Jerusalem rather than at Shiloh, gave to the Judean patois made use of in the service, the sanction of a holy language, and it became forever thereafter the standard of the best literary style, thus raising, in literature at least, a break-water against the rising tide of Aramaism. After the upheaval in the national life occasioned by the secession of the ten tribes, the result of dissatisfaction in the tribes of the north with the growing power of Judah and the centralizing policy of the court faction in Jerusalem, the Israelite kingdom was by the necessities of its situation, drawn into close and almost constant alliance with the petty Aramaic

States of the Anti-Lebanon. The effect of this alliance could not but be reflected in the spoken dialect of the northern kingdom which had ere the final invasion and conquest by Salmanu âsir (שַׁלְמַנְאֶסֶר Shalmaneser, 722 B. C.) been lost to Hebrew speech and at least in the patois of the common people become Aramaic. The question which has so vexed many good people as to the whereabouts of the lost ten tribes, recognized within a decade in peoples as dissimilar as the American Indians and the Afghans, seems to me capable of easy solution by the probable fact that the great mass of them never left Palestine. The peculiarly Assyrian policy of securing themselves from revolt and internal disorder seems not to have extended to the deportation of entire peoples, but was as effectively accomplished by the removal of the upper and governing classes; in some few cases it extended to the middle classes, probably never to the peasantry. How far this deportation went in the case of the ten tribes we have no sure information; but probably the great mass of the people were not disturbed. Those who were taken captive and settled in Mesopotamia, either filtered back amidst the Jewish returns in the age of Cyrus and thereafter, or preferring the Euphrates valley became there, with their Jewish brethren who had chosen to remain rather than to undergo the peril and hardship of founding a new State, (became there, I say), the nucleus of those Babylonian communities whose literary and commercial activity is in a later time so celebrated. Out of the mixture of the foreign peoples brought into the upland of Ephraim, with those who had remained there of the Israelites, there grew up that cultus, so distasteful to the Jews, whose centre was Gerizim, and the local patois—in all its main features the old Ephraimite—which developed into what is known to us as the Samaritan. The Galilean country was settled by a more mixed population, the outcome of which was an Aramaic dialect with such an obscure pronunciation of certain characteristic Shemitic sounds, that we are told in the Talmud that it was impossible to understand a certain Galilean who came to the Jerusalem market to purchase something, whether he desired to have חְמָר (hamâr) an ass, חֲמַר (hamar) wine, עֲמַר (amar) some wool, or אִמַּר (immar) a lamb, all pronounced precisely the same in his patois. It is this thick pronunciation, almost a brogue, which is the point in the betrayal of Peter by his speech. I fear I weary you by philological detail, and can plead as my only excuse that most of the misconception, shall I add preconception of the present day, as to the Old Testament has its origin just here. Bear in mind then if you please that by the end of the seventh century before our era the old language of Canaan had probably ceased to be a spoken tongue north of Jerusalem; the exact linguistic line being of course a changing one and impossible of definition. In the middle belt of Ephraim was spoken a patois whose historical development is the Samaritan; in the further north there was gradually crystallizing out of many elements the later Galilean.

We have thus traced the Hebrew to its extinction as a spoken dialect amongst the great majority of those to whom it had once been a mother tongue; let us now glance at its fate in the kingdom of Judah. The little kingdom of Judah, notwithstanding the foreign policy of its court, (who, forgetting that their very strength lay in their weakness and isolation, constantly sought the alliance and aped the luxurious manners of the great powers), despite the dissoluteness of morals among the people, who not only accepted, but sought after the cultus of the Arameans, had in the Temple and learned classes of Jerusalem a principle of stability for its literature, and so, to a great extent, for its language, which had failed the northern kingdom. At the time of the attack on Jerusalem by Sennacherib (Sanherib כנחריב) we know that the courtiers of Hezekiah understood Aramaic, which at that time was the cultured and diplomatic language of the Orient—somewhat as the French in

Europe during the last century. We also know that it was not understood by the common people, who still retained the older Canaanite tongue, which had come to be called, as the dialect of the other tribes had become Aramaic, specifically the " dialect of Judah," all of which you may see by referring to Isaiah xxxvi. 11. There is scarce another so widely accepted belief as to the history of the East, founded on so radical an error, as that of the loss of their language by the Jews during the captivity. This is convincingly disproven by the fact that the dialect spoken by them at a later day could not have been acquired in Assyria, but being precisely of a kind with that spoken by their neighbors on the north, must have come to the Jews from them. The Captivity, with its breaking down of all authority and religion, left the peasantry no doubt exposed to Aramaic influences from the people who surrounded them, but the educated and governing classes, who were carried away into Mesopotamia, lived together in dense colonies, and would have little occasion, as they doubtless had small disposition, to acquire the tongue of their conquerors. At all events, they did *not* acquire it.[1] Some of the Psalms written during

---

[1] The author here assumes, and probably rightly, that there is no good ground for the assertion made by some writers that Aramaic had in the days of the Exile ousted the vernacular, and come to be the spoken

the Exile show as exquisitely delicate a perception of the niceties of the language as those of the earlier time. It seems impossible they should have been composed among a people who were rapidly losing their language. The Jews did not lose their language until several centuries later; the main, in fact almost the sole effect of the Exile was in preparing the way for the subsequent change by breaking down their nationality and bringing them as subjects under powers whose official language continued to be Aramaic until almost the opening of our era. The exulants, who return to Palestine, bring back with them their old speech; in fact, with a generation present at the foundation of the latter Temple, whose memory extended back to the former, it seems to me impossible that any great change should have taken place.

The writings of the post-exilic period in the clearness and ease of their style, attest the language as a living and spoken one; further and immediately to our point, the writings of the post-exilic religious orators or prophets, which would have been of no value unless generally understood by the mass of the people, are written in the purest vernacular. The linguistic tenacity of the Jewish people is something which interests scholars in very many fields—the

language of Babylon and Babylonia. The opinion that it was the tongue of the Chaldeans is now entirely abandoned. (T.)

Jewish universities on the Euphrates preserve to us forms which the contemporaneous Arabic had long out-grown; Spanish scholars tell us that the writings of the Spanish Jews (in Spanish) are in a style two centuries older than their time; and there may be found in the dialects of the French and German Jews many forms, preserved almost like flies in amber, from the very oldest French and German. It was the same tenacity which helped the Jewish people to retain their old language, for three centuries after their return, under constant Aramaizing influence. It is not to our purpose to follow minutely the decay of Jewish speech, beginning with the peasantry, and last of all reaching the religious orders; it extended through the Persian dominion, during the feuds of the Greek dynasties, when Palestine hung, the apple of discord between the warring generals of Alexander, and not until the repressive measures of the Seleucidæ to "damp the speech of sedition," does it entirely cease to be a spoken language in the second century before our era—crushed out between the upper and nether millstones of Greek and Aramaic. Its history henceforth, is that of a learned language, one of the schools and not of common life. The Jews of the Greek dispersion learned Greek, and so completely forgot the mother tongue that a Greek translation of their sacred books had to be made for them. Those who remained in Palestine, together with the settlements of the exiles who had tarried in Babylonia, spoke Aramaic, until this was, in the sixth century after our era, dispossessed in turn by the Arabic. The subsequent history of the dialects of the Jews and the rise of the Rabbinic and the new Hebrew, does not, interesting though it be, fall within the scope of these lectures.

I trust that I have thus far made clear to you that the so-called Hebrew is the tongue of Palestine where we can trace it back to a period two thousand years before our era; that it was displaced among the northern ten tribes by the Aramaic in the seventh century before our era; among the Jews it was retained until the second; that since this time it has been a purely learned language, spoken indeed after a fashion, but without growth, or hold on popular consciousness. So far from being a mysterious language, it is one of the easiest for the scholar to grasp and determine the position of. You will notice that what I have said of the "tongue of Canaan" has been confined to it as spoken by the Israelites. It is with intent that I have not alluded to it as spoken by the Phenicians, or the other lowland people; that would lead us too far from the main point we have in view, without changing in any essential particular the history of the language as we have sketched it. Let us turn now from the linguistic to the literary side on which, hereafter, in these lectures, I shall chiefly dwell.

The literature of the Jewish people falls naturally into two almost equal divisions, the literature written in their own native dialect—the Hebrew—and the literature written by them in foreign languages. The latter, which by the very terms of these lectures is excluded from our present attention, is a literature of enormous extent, principally preserved in the Aramaic and Arabic, but found beside in almost all the civilized languages of the ancient and modern world. It contains many of the writings which have done most to give renown to Jewish literature; in Greek, the philosophy of Philo and the Jewish fore-runners of the new Platonism in Alexandria; in the Aramaic the main part of the Talmud, hugest yet crudest of all encyclopedias, a very sea of learning which swamps most of the craft which venture upon it; in the Arabic, the poetry and belles-lettres of the Spanish Jews, which lent grace to the civilization of the Caliphate of Cordova, while Christian Europe lay in barbarism.

Leaving this and taking up the Jewish literature written in Hebrew, we find this again falling naturally into two divisions—the literature written during the existence of the Hebrew as a spoken language—the natural outgrowth and expression of the thought and

3

life of the people, and the literature written after the Hebrew had ceased to be a spoken language—the artificial product of reflection and scholastic effort. This latter we are obliged once more to exclude from our field of view. Suffice it to say in passing, it is an extensive literature, whose chief value is technical, for grammatical investigation and the like. The artificiality and conceits of style with which it endeavors to atone for lack of originality renders so much of it as lays any claim to be pure literature cloying to the taste and almost unreadable.

It is the native literature during the life of the spoken language with which alone we are concerned at this time. We have already seen that the Hebrew was a spoken language for about two thousand years, from a period somewhat prior to the twentieth century before our era until the beginning of the second century. The limits of the literary period agree in the main with this; perhaps, however, it were better on account of the great variance of opinion as to the date of the later writings of the Hebrew Scripture, to state the literary period more in gross—as from the beginning of the Hebrew language until the opening of our era. You have thus, I trust, a clear idea of what the first period of Hebrew literature—that with which these lectures are occupied—is. It is the period of the literature during the life of the spoken language, extending over two thousand years, from the twentieth century until our era.

When we ask what are the written remains of this period we find them of three kinds: (1) certain inscriptions and coins, (2) a few apocryphal books, and (3), and mainly, the collection of writings known to us as the Hebrew Scriptures.

The inscriptions are some twenty or more carved seals and gems, some of which belong to a period long prior to the Exile, and of which Dr. Levy of Breslau has treated at length. For paleography they are of immense interest, but as they contain nothing but proper names can scarcely be reckoned as literature.

The coins are those of the Maccabean dynasty, and are all subsequent to the year 135 before our era: Though of great rarity and numismatic value, they are too late to throw any light on the language or literature. Their Hebrew legends prove no more than the Latin now stamped on the coinage of England.

What I mean by Apocryphal books I doubt my being able to make clear until I speak of the collection of the Hebrew literature and the reasons which lead to its division into so called canonical and apocryphal writings:—for the moment then this may remain in abeyance.

We have remaining the Hebrew Scriptures now in our hands, by far the most extensive, practically the only remains, we have of Hebrew literature from its first period. I have said only remains. They were far from being the only literature during this period, for we have fragments scattered all through the writings which have come to us of a popular and religious poetry now irrecoverably lost; while the compilers of the Hebrew annals with most painstaking accuracy give us the literary sources from which they draw their information, and refer us to books circulating in their day for a fulness of detail which they themselves have not space to give. Look in any introduction to the Hebrew Scriptures and you will find full citations of this literature. "The Book of the Wars of the Lord;" "The Book of the Just;" "Chronicles of the Prophet Nathan;" "Prophecy of Ahia the Shilonite;" "Chronicles of the Reign of David." The literature which has survived necessarily presupposes a flourishing contemporaneous literature in a high degree of cultivation, and of a literary reading class in the Jewish community.

When we take up these fragments of the early literature which have come down to us in the Hebrew Scripture, the first thing staring the student of the original in the face is the precise similarity of grammatical form running through the entirety of the writings. I presume you know that grammatical form in all literary investigation, be it even in our own English, is regarded as the most trustworthy indication of the age of any piece of literature at issue. An English scholar will at a glance distinguish the English of Chaucer from that of the age of Jonson by its form. When we take up the Hebrew Scripture purporting to be a collection of fragments from a period of over two thousand years, we find from the oldest to the youngest, a precise similarity of form; no archaisms from an older time, no trace of growth, still less of decay—a phenomenon unparalleled in literary history—a language apparently sprung full clothed from the brain of a people who continued to speak it for twenty centuries unchanged. This has been made the basis of many charges of designed manufacture of the writings to serve the purpose of a priestly caste who gained control of the rehabilitated Jewish state shortly after the Exile. There is no other human speech or literature without a history—were the form in which we have the Jewish literature the original one, there would be strong reason for suspicion that it was the product of a single age and school. We know, however, that we do not have the sacred literature of the Jews in its original form, but in the liturgical shape into which it was cast for purposes of worship by certain professors of the University of Tiberias in Galilee, about the sixth century of our era.

Perhaps I may make it clear to you by an example from English literature. Imagine that the entirety of English literature, from Cædmon to Spenser, with all the variety and growth of form which enables us to distinguish it into *old, middle,* and *new English,* had, in the age of Anne, been cast by the Anglican clergy into a form suitable to the intoned reading of their service, and in that shape alone had come down to us. You will perceive that to be understood by the people of the reign of Anne, the forms which had become archaic in their time must be given up;—to suit it to the intoned reading, the original sounds must receive an unnatural and artificial pronunciation. We should possess the early literature of England, no doubt, with unchanged credibility and historical interest, but we should have lost all the landmarks for determining its growth—it would be early English literature in the language of the time of Anne. We should have lost beside the only sure clue to determining the age of the writings, whose authorship was for any reason in dispute. The history of English literature could only be gathered from allusions in the writings themselves to places, persons or events, that we knew, from the contemporaneous literature of other peoples which were not so evilly entreated, had lived or occurred in some one period or another. Probably, however, if we wrote English literary history we should form some subjective and dogmatic standard in our minds as to how it should have been developed, and then with as much literary skill as we were capable of, fit its remains to this Procrustean bed of our ideal.

Such is precisely the condition in which the Hebrew writings have come to us. The liturgical revision of the Tiberian theologians has obliterated all the distinctive forms of the earlier time. The language of Moses is similar to that of Isaiah, and that of Isaiah to Malachi, all being in common flattened out into the low (of course I mean in the sense we say low Dutch) pronunciation in vogue in Tiberias in the sixth century subsequent to our era. Bear in mind what I said as to the supposed case in early English. We have the old Hebrew literature with unchanged credibility and historical value; what it has lost is its original literary form. So you may understand why Hebrew literature has furnished ground for opinions as to its origin and development, so diametrically opposed to one another. Approaching it from the purely literary side, scholars whose learning can not be called in question, have referred its beginning to periods as remote from one another as Moses and Ezra, and there is scarce one of its writings the opinions as to whose origin does not range over several centuries. Subjective standards have indeed been raised and vehemently insisted on by the varying schools, for the very reason that there is not in the writings themselves that sure standard of literary form which alone enables scholars to trace the development of any literature and establish beyond controversy the age of its several writings.[1]

The beginnings of the literature of Israel are coincident with the beginnings of its national consciousness at the time of Moses. Compared with other literatures of the Orient, it is of comparatively recent origin. The pyramids which to-day look down on us had, when Moses was born, been keeping watch over Egypt for five[2] centuries, and the heyday of Egyptian literature and culture had long before him begun to wane. Even in the Shemitic people there had been a long period of literary development, and to the eyes of the western nations there has in this century been unearthed a literature written by the Chaldean ancestors of Abraham.

Drawing the line again more closely we find even in the "language of Canaan," clear traces of a literature prior to the Mosaic age, for when, forty years

[1] That the author does not here mean to exclude wholly other notes of age than the phonetic-grammatical of which he speaks, is evident from the judgments he passes pp. 62, 131, on the dates of various Old Testament writers. His object is to warn against arbitrary subjective critical conclusions, and to insist on a strict scientific critical method. (T.)

[2] Leading Egyptologists assign to the oldest of the pyramids a much greater antiquity even than this. (T.)

later Israel enters Canaan there is mention of a city so celebrated by its library as to have been named after it.[1] Doubtless, even the tribal fragments out of which Israel was welded into a nation, had their own traditions, some of which may have been committed to writing. We find throughout the Genesis constant evidence of the use of older material, partially explainable as transmitted by verbal tradition, as the refrain from the sword-song of Lamech; but in a measure, only explainable, as the old chronicle in chap. xiv. by being preserved in some written shape. In the strict sense of the word, however, we have no trace of a distinct literary activity, in any of the peoples who made up Israel prior to the beginning of their national existence. It is a literary problem of the greatest moment, just how much of the literature which the pious reflection of a later generation refers to its eponymous lawgiver, can justly be given to him. The discussion of the origin of the Mosaic literature would in itself involve many lectures. I am fully aware with what force and learning the objections to the Mosaic origin of the Hebrew literature both have been and are being urged. Perhaps that which is most celebrated and widely accepted among scholars at the present day, is the one presented with great lucidity by Kuenen in his "Re-

---

[1] Kirjath-sepher, "City of books." Josh. xv. 15. (T.)

ligion of Israel," that the beginnings of Jewish literature were the prophetic writings of the eighth century. To me it seems impossible that the literature of any people should have writings like those of the eighth century for its incunabula.[1] If the canons gained from the study of other literatures be of any value, these eighth century writings, now so much discussed, are inexplicable save as the ripe fruitage of a long previous literary period. It is impossible, however, for even the most conservative student of the Mosaic literature, to deny that in its present shape it shows such traces of editing and annotation, as to render it inconceivable that it should have come from any one man or any one time. Into the so-called theory of manuscripts, with whose painful minutiæ the Hitzigian school first confused their readers, and then befogged themselves, I do not now propose to enter. The fairest summing up of the outcome of the whole discussion, is probably this; that the Mosaic literature in its main lines, its documents, its genealogies, and its laws, is the product of the great mind who laid the foundation of the Jewish state; that it first passed from documentary to liter-

[1] Kuenen holds that none of the present books of the Old Testament were committed to writing before the eighth century, but admits a preceding unwritten literature, assigning the Song of Deborah, for example, to the period of the Judges. (Religion of Israel, English Translation, i. 313, 314.) (T.)

ary shape, after the rise of the Jewish kingdom had given the order and leisure necessary to literature, and finally was edited after the Exile by those who collected the canon, with annotations on many points of interest to their time, which in the original were obscure. This to me adequately explains all the phenomena which these writings offer, and I am unable to perceive either on scholarly or literary grounds sufficient warrant for the more radical theories.

The period of the entry into Canaan, of its conquest and gradual occupation, was one of anarchy and unrest, such as produces among most peoples myths and ballads, but rarely sustained and consecutive literature. Its products in Israel are war songs like that of Deborah, fables, like that of Jotham, narratives, current in the mouth of the people, of their heroes and warriors, like Samson and Jephthah.

First after the establishment of internal quiet through the Davidic kingdom, together with the setting up of the Temple and court in Jerusalem, did there grow up any literary class, or a literature in our sense of the word. There seems early to have been attached to the court stated officials, called chroniclers, who were doubtless the compilers of many of the books—such as "Chronicles of the Reign of David," which are quoted from or referred to in the works which remain to us. There was another class called "keepers of the archives," whose duty, no doubt, was the collection and preservation not only of the earlier written laws and documents, but also the traditions of the wilderness and those disordered years of the conquest which were fast fading from men's minds. It was from these collections that the books of Joshua and Judges were edited, by whom we know not, in the times of the early kings.

With the luxury and culture of the reign of Solomon came a contact with and knowledge of foreign literatures, from which arose a branch of literature in the Hebrew which seems almost exclusively confined to the Solomonic times, that of translations. The book of Job, which I shall speak of at a later time, and many chapters of the Proverbs come under this head.

Poetry was the earliest, and it continued until the extinction of the language to be the most exquisite flowering of its literature. Much of the poetry which comes from pre-Davidic times—the Blessing of Jacob —the Song by the Sea—the Song of Deborah—is as perfect in form as, and perhaps even more forcible in language than any of the later poetry. But it was first with the establishment of the liturgical worship and orders of singers in the temple that Hebrew poetry assumed its most characteristic form in the religious song. We shall hereafter see that somewhat more than half of the poems remaining to us in the Book of Psalms were written during the duration of the Judean kingdom.

Prophetic literature had its origin in the schools of the Prophets—communities half ascetic, half religious, which have existed in the orient with different names, under every form of religion, from the earliest times until the present. It is the characteristic literature of the period of the Kings, but I must defer its more general consideration until I come to speak of Isaiah. Its representatives in this period are Joel (870), Jonah (800), Amos (790), Hosea (785), Micah (725), Isaiah (717), Nahum (700), Zephaniah (640), Habakkuk (604), Obadiah (?), Jeremiah running into the Exile.

Of the profane literature of this period, which we have evidence was an extensive one, there is naught preserved to us save perhaps it be the Song of Songs, or Song of Solomon, in regard to which many of the Church Fathers held the view now far from uncommon among scholars, that it is a popular drama which some strange chance of tradition or editing had brought into its present place.

The golden period of Jewish letters ends with the Exile. From the post-exilic times we have literature perfect in form, and classical in language; but the evident imitation of antique models, and the constant striving to conceal, through finished shape, the dearth of originality, betray it to us as a literary aftermath.

We have already seen that the upper, the writing and reading class, were those who most suffered from the Exile. On their return to their old home, immediately after ensuring their own safety, there naturally came the desire to secure what was most sacred to them from their early literature, in some permanent form, lest a new catastrophe might utterly obliterate it. Whether it were Ezra, to whom the unanimity of tradition points, or his contemporaries in the so-called great Synagogue who inaugurated this movement, we do not know. All the writings were not collected at once, but gradually through several centuries and in three separate collections, in which they still remain in the original.

The first endeavor seems to have been to secure the remains of the Mosaic writings, the most venerable and sacred literary heritage of the nation. These were collected almost immediately upon the return, and becoming the religious and political constitution of the new State, have retained for Israel ever since an importance so much greater than that of the rest of its literature, as almost to place them in a category of their own. The remnant of Ephraim, who somewhat later, with motives not unmixed, offered aid to the returned colony, and were alienated for all time

COLLECTION OF THE HEBREW WRITINGS. 63

by the refusal, accept alone as sacred the Mosaic writings in the form in which they were collected at this time.

The Mosaic writings, as those first collected, stand at the beginning of all our Bibles as they do in the original. Their final editing and arrangement in five books—in fact the whole literary shape in which we now have them is the work of this period. Only the chapters and verses in our English Bibles are of late origin, and these, in some cases, are subsequent to the Protestant Reformation. The name we give these writings—Pentateuch—and that of their divisions— Genesis, Exodus, etc., either come directly or are translations from the Septuagint, a Greek translation made in the second century before our era, as tradition informs us, for one of the Ptolemies, who secured for the Alexandrian library, somewhat as Professor Müller is now striving to do for Oxford, a collection of translations from the chief religious books of the world. The name in the original Mosaic literature is תּוֹרָה *Tora*, one of the many Bedouin words preserved by the Israelites from their nomadic days. It means some landmark, be it a tree, a rock, a ruin, by which the traveller traces his way through a trackless wild; hence in the ethical sense the land-mark set to guide men on the way of life— unfortunately translated ὁ νόμος in the Greek of the New Testament—whence we have our name, "The Law."

No sooner was this collection completed than there seems to have come the popular impulse to gather and preserve the writings of the men whose memories were held sacred by them from the former time, and to put in some permanent and compendious form the history of the Davidic kingdom with its departed glories. The result of this was a second collection called נְבִיאִים *Nebiim*, a name whose force is obscured to us through the unfortunate translation of the Greek οἱ προφῆται—The Prophets.

A prophet, as we shall see hereafter, was, and still is in Shemitic conception, any holy man who comes with a divine message—we should not be far from right were we to paraphrase the original as, "Writings of the Saints."

From the pre-exilic time, they received into this collection, the writings of Joel, Amos, Hosea, Isaiah, Micah, Zephaniah, Nahum, Habakkuk, Obadiah, also Jeremiah, whose activities as writer and orator extend into exilic times. We can also readily understand the reason for the acceptance of Ezekiel who belongs wholly to the Exile, and whose rhetoric clearly betrays his Babylonian surrounding; the reason of the acceptance of Haggai and Zechariah, one an old man through whom the prophetic spirit had come down from the former time, the other the messenger to the new state, is none the less plain. It is not clear why Jonah should have been included.

This collection was probably not completed until a number of years after the Exile, as it includes an anonymous prophecy, made by one who calls himself the messenger of Jehovah — Malachi — a designation and not a proper name, and which is usually referred to a period somewhat subsequent to Nehemiah. Observe that the book of Daniel is not found in this original prophetic collection. According to all Jewish canonical tradition, it is a much later book, and in the Hebrew text is found in a collection of writings which was not inaugurated until after the prophetic collection had been closed. Daniel has come into its position among the Prophets, in our English Scripture, from the Greek translation, which, I fear, the scholars of King James' time were somewhat more conversant with than with the Hebrew original. The arrangement of books in this collection (at least in the form we have it preserved to us) is partly chronological, but in the main regulated by size;—thus there come first Isaiah, Jeremiah and Ezekiel, though none of them are as early as some of the so called minor prophets. When we follow further the same collection and inquire into the arrangement of the twelve minor writings, we find Hosea immediately following Ezekiel, and in turn followed by Joel and Amos, merely on the principle of comparative bulk. Haggai, Zechariah and Malachi were placed at the end, for reasons purely chronological, after the rest of the collection had been made up. We can not now see any clear or consistent reason for the position of Obadiah, Jonah, Micah, Nahum, Habakkuk, and Zephaniah, which stand together in the middle of the collection. Probably for the most part synchronous with the making up of this collection there was being gathered the material for the ancestral history from the close of the Mosaic literature until the breaking up of the Exile. The collectors, whoever they may be, possessed ready to their hand the writings, named from the period they cover, Joshua and Judges, which we have already seen were compiled in the preceding age from the royal archives. These they made use of in their existing form. They seem then to have addressed themselves to preparing a history of the people to cover the gap which remained, from the last of Judges until the Exile. In doing this they evidently make use of all the material available to them, not only the archives and chronicles which had been saved from the Assyrian invasions, but even the very traditions and songs which lingered in the mouths of the people. The result is a work whose style and consecution betray the offspring of single effort, but which for later reasons of convenience has been separated into four parts, 1st and 2nd Samuel and 1st and 2nd Kings—these names, which often, by the way, vary, being meant as in the case of Joshua and Judges, to indicate the subject and not the author of the book. Chronicles, which is adjacent in our English Bibles, is a much later book. It is the product of a school of thought and an historical method almost diametrically opposed to the one which has given us this earlier history. In the original Hebrew, Chronicles stands at the very end of the last collection of writings, which could hardly have been made until some centuries later. The annals thus completed from the older writings Joshua and Judges, and the new compend of the subsequent history, were not set in a separate collection, but placed one might almost say as an introductory historical preface, to the writings of the worthies of this same period which had already been collected. To the whole collection was given the name of its chief part—" The Writings of the Saints "—seemingly confirming what I have just remarked, that the historical part was regarded as secondary; perhaps no more than an historical sketch of the time in which lived and acted those whose writings it was the main end of the collection to preserve and hand down to the after time. In the original this second collection is placed with correctness immediately after the Mosaic literature. The arrangement in our English Bibles represents an endeavor borrowed from some of the old versions to group the writings topically rather than historically.

After the collection, both of the Mosaic literature and of the prophetic writings had been completed, there was still a remainder of writings, hallowed in the affections of the people, which did not come from the Mosaic time, neither were they by prophetic authors. So by the canon which had been set up in the two former collections they were of necessity excluded from them. These were gathered in the third and last collection, which received the name כְּתוּבִים — *Kethubim*, writings—or, as the Greek aptly paraphrases it, ἁι ἁγίαι γραφαί—"The Hagiographa"—"Holy Writings." From the pre-exilic times there was received into it, first of all, such portions of the Psalms as were then existing, which were from a great variety of authors; the Book of Job, whose author was unknown, and which was probably an adaptation from some foreign literature; the collection of Proverbs, including not only Jewish, but also Edomite and Arabic proverbial sayings—(as you may assure yourself by looking at the later chapters)—and the Lamentations, wrung from some pious heart by the desolations of the city of his worship. A slight gap in the previous history between Judges and Samuel is supplied by the little book of Ruth, scarcely as much history, as it is the most exquisite of pastoral idyls. A new historical book, unfortunately severed in twain in a later day, and known to us as Ezra and Nehemiah, was written to preserve the story of the later uprising of the Jewish State, and to complete the historical narrative of the earlier books. Thus the collection at the beginning of the fourth century probably included Psalms, Proverbs, Job, Lamentations, Ruth, and the Ezra books. Unlike the other collections, this was not then closed, but remained open to receive both the writings of a later time and some earlier ones, whose sanctity and value first became established during the succeeding two centuries. Among the later writings are clearly to be placed Esther, the reason of whose right in the collection is still in dispute among scholars, and the Chronicles, founded on the Temple records and a mass of documents, unused or inaccessible to the compilers of the previous history of the same period. I have said already that Chronicles stands the last book of the Hebrew original—who the author was we do not know—he seems often overmastered by his matter, and some have gained the impression in reading him that he is writing in an imperfectly acquired language.

Of early literature which was not till late received in the collection is the Song of Songs—a book whose sacred character remains until this day an undecided subject of inquiry. It was one of the burning questions of Jewish theology in the first century of our era, whether it might be read with washen or unwashen hands; *i. e.*, whether it was sacred or profane.

There remain but two books more, Daniel and Ecclesiastes. The opinions as to the age of these books are now very widely variant; for Daniel, from the Exile to the persecution of Antiochus Epiphanes; for Ecclesiastes, that it is a reflection of the aged Solomon, or a Stoic pamphlet of the year 50. The views of both positive and negative critics are held on grounds of dogmatic prepossession which will not bear literary criticism. It is impossible, I imagine, while men's minds are unable to investigate these books without the present prejudice, to determine with accuracy either their age or their authorship.

When this collection of "Holy Writings" was closed is not known, and must be largely determined by the dates we assign to its later books. We know with reasonable surety that it existed in its present shape at the beginning of our era. In the New Testment the collection is called the Psalms, a name taken from its principal book;—the reference to the

COLLECTION OF THE HEBREW WRITINGS. 71

Law, the Prophets and the Psalms being an allusion to the three-fold collection in the Hebrew Scriptures, which was then as it is now in existence. In the arrangement of the several writings in this collection, there is a great divergence even between the manuscripts of the original—a reflection of the uncertainty prevailing until a time subsequent to our era as to the age and authority of one or more of the books. The more common arrangement in our best printed editions of the original is: Psalms, Proverbs, Job, Song of Songs, Ruth, Lamentations, Ecclesiastes, Esther, Daniel, Ezra, Nehemiah, Chronicles.

This arrangement is topical—First, three poetical books, then five so called מְגִלּוֹת *Megilloth*, or Rolls— read by the later Synagogue on certain feast-days: the Song of Songs at the Passover; Ruth at Pentecost (Whitsuntide); Lamentations on the anniversary of the Temple Burning; Ecclesiastes at Tabernacles, and the most prized of all, Esther on Purim, often no more than a Saturnalia, and lastly, the four historical books.

As to Ruth and Lamentations there is some reason for supposing that at one time they may have belonged to the older collection of prophets; at a later period, for a certain convenience in the arrangement of the synagogue reading lessons, which I cannot pause to explain, they were transferred hither from their original position. All the other writings just named clearly belong in this last collection. Their position in our version is borrowed from the somewhat eclectic arrangement of Ptolemy's translators.

Thus we have finished our brief sketch of the Hebrew language, of its early literature, and of its collection. The name this literature is wont to receive is "canonical," *i. e.*, in conformity to some standard which is set up. I had desired to explain what this standard was and how it led to the rejection as apocryphal, viz. : for private and not public reading—of a number of valuable and instructive writings disapproved of, mayhap, because unread, by many who were contemporaneous with the later books of the canonical collection. I will not broach the question now, for the closing hour leaves me insufficient space to satisfactorily discuss it. At some time ere I conclude these lectures I will take an opportunity to further speak of it to you.

LECTURE III.

AFTER considering in my first lecture the position of the Shemitic peoples and languages, I endeavored in my second hour to sketch for you in most hasty outline the history of the Hebrew people and their language, of their literature and its collection. I have been asked to make more clear to some of you our sources of information as to the three collections of which I then spoke—The Mosaic writings, or Pentateuch —"The Writings of the Saints," known to us as " Prophets "—and the *Kethubim* (Hagiographa) or miscellaneous writings. None of you need be appalled at my suggesting your confirming what I then said by looking in any printed Hebrew Bible, for, in the better editions, the indexes and rubrics are all printed in Latin. You will find the arrangement to be precisely as I stated.

You will also trust me when I say to you that the manuscripts contain in all respects a similar arrangement. But some one may say, may it not be an arrangement peculiar to the occidental manuscripts on which our printed versions of the Hebrew are based, none of which as we well know are older than the twelfth century? This is possible, as the western manuscripts have many arrangements both of books and text peculiar to themselves, but if you will come with me to St. Petersburg, I will show you Hebrew manuscripts of a school whose principles of text and arrangement are radically diverse from those of the Tiberian school from whom our western manuscripts have come. Rescued within a decade from the cellars of a certain Firkowitzsh of Kschefet Kali in the Crimea, (whose being a rabbi did not prevent his turning an honest penny at forging,) these so-called Babylonian codices, reaching back to the first century, are a treasure to the Russian Imperial Museum, even more unique and valuable than the famous Sinaitic manuscript of the New Testament. In these again we find the three collections in an order exactly parallel to that in our western manuscripts. Now an arrangement common to the manuscripts of both these schools cannot well be younger than the dispersion of the Jewish scholars consequent on the Roman invasions at the taking of Jerusalem by Titus; or the greater dispersion of fifty years later when Hadrian crushed out in a bloody massacre the last hope of national independence which had shown itself in the foolhardy sedition of the fanatic Simeon bar-Kokhba.

Thus we have manuscript evidence for saying that these three collections existed in the original as early as our era. In the time of Christ we know they existed, for He speaks of the Old Testament, not as a whole, but as existing in three separate collections. The Greek, through which we have His words, but in a mirror from the original, makes Him say the Law, the Prophets, and the Psalms; there can be no doubt, however, that He Himself as a Jew, speaking to Jews, would use the very designations I mentioned in the last hour.

But one more supposition can be left to the objector, and that is that the arrangement in use by the Jews at the opening of our era was one made for convenience in the Synagogue worship—a sort of lesson book, as it were, while the Greek Septuagint translation, almost two centuries older, has really an earlier arrangement of the books which has, with wisdom, been borrowed by the Vulgate and by our English version. Fortunately we have evidence of these three collections being in existence, which is contemporaneous with, if not earlier than the translation of the Septuagint.

The Wisdom of Jesus Sirach is the most important of the so-called Apocryphal writings, and one, the reason of whose exclusion from the canon, while a book like Esther is admitted, is hard to see even on religious grounds. Its author lived in the third century. We have it preserved in the Greek translation alone, prepared by the piety of his grandson, about the middle of the second century, and in Egypt, the very home of the Septuagint. In the preface to this Greek translation his grandson speaks constantly of, and refers to, as well known, the three collections of the national literature under precisely the same names by which we know them now. The evidence, therefore, is conclusive, and I have endeavored to clinch it on purely objective grounds, without referring either to the Talmud in which it is recognized as of long standing in its time, the fifth century, A.D., or to the unanimous consensus among Shemitic scholars, whose opinion is worth the quoting, to its undoubted originality and to the eclecticism of arrangement in the translation of the Septuagint, which our English version has followed. The object of these lectures is not to broach novel theories or suggest any new arrangement of Hebrew Literature. However remote from your ordinary consciousness some of the views here stated may be, they are in every case what has seemed to me a fair summing up of the researches of those scholars who have devoted themselves to the investigation of this literature.

Let us now turn to that part of this early Hebrew literature which will occupy our attention during the next few lectures :

"THE BOOK OF PSALMS,"

and on consideration I have deemed it better to gather in the form of lectures the points of greatest interest as to its collection, arrangement and authorship, rather than take up the more technical exposition of some of the poems which, I imagine, would be of less interest and value to the majority of my hearers.

As I have already said, the "Psalm Book" has its proper historical position as the opening book of the third and last collection of the early literature of the Jews—the *Kethubim* or "Miscellaneous Writings." That it stood there in the early time is clear from the naming of the entire collection of these writings as "Psalms" in the New Testament, a method of naming a book or collection after its first part which is found until this day in the orient, and is familiar to every scholar (so in Philo and II Maccabees).

It is no argument against this that in the so-called Spanish Manuscripts, as in the Masora, Chronicles precedes, as it was placed there on the purely subjective ground that the collection might begin with the genealogy from Adam; while similar in kind is the reason of the Talmudic arrangement of Ruth before Psalms—that the Davidic songs might be preceded by a sketch of David's ancestors. We have seen that its position in our version is unfortunately borrowed from the topical arrangement adopted for easy reference by the scholars of Ptolemy, in the early Greek translation prepared by them for the great library of the Museum at Alexandria, whose books by the way had all heated the baths of the fanatical bishop Theophilus two centuries before the Caliph Omar or Amru the Arab conqueror of Egypt was born. Of course you know the very good, though apocryphal story of Omar's reply, "If the books are in accord with the Koran they are useless—if not they are heretical, so in any case to be destroyed."

The name our version gives this collection is "The Book of Psalms." This is not however the name the collection bears in the original—it is there called תְהִלִים *Tehillim*, תִּלִּים, *Tillim*, Aramaic תִּלִּין, *Tillin*, Praises, *i. e.*, Songs of Praises, or Praise Book. This name Praise Book I had thought it almost too self-evident to say, had not my attention been called to a misapprehension on this very point since last we met, was first given by the final editors and compilers of this collection, whoever they may have been. In fact, the titles of all the books of the Hebrew

Scriptures are from the hand of the editor rather than the author. This is shown very clearly by the great variance of these titles among the older manuscripts of the original; moreover the utter dissimilarity of the oldest versions from the original in the matter of titles, indicates that there was in the early time nothing sacred in them nor any authoritative tradition. If ever any of my hearers come to have the pleasure and toil of studying oriental letters, they will find that the title of his work is that which the author elaborates with most loving devotion. As the Arabs say, it is the cord on which he hangs the pearls of his rhetoric. So there can be little doubt that each of these several books had at one time some distinctive title of its own.

A few traces of such older titles are still found embodied in the text and treated there as the first verse of the book: Habbakuk i. 1., Nahum, i. 1., Obadiah 1., Micah, i. 1., etc., though here there rises again in every case, the question as to whether this or that particular title be from the author or his first editor.

If we had the titles which the authors themselves gave their works, they would doubtless possess the same credibility and historical authority, be it less or greater, which we predicate of the works themselves. What we now have, or rather, call titles are scarcely more than very late descriptive headlines, and a plainly editorial device for helping the memory and facilitating the reading of the rolls. I need not enter upon or endeavor to explain the almost endless diversity of these titles both in the original and its early translations. As they exist in our English King James, eleven of them are borrowed from versions other than the original. Of these so-called titles, twenty-two are names of persons, either, as in the case of Isaiah, Jeremiah, Ezekiel, Hosea, Joel, Amos, Obadiah, Jonah, Micah, Nahum, Habakkuk, Zephaniah, Haggai, and Zechariah, the authors of the writings, or, as in the case of Joshua, Ruth, Samuel, Ezra, Nehemiah, Esther, Job and Daniel, the heroes of the period the book describes. Malachi should be reckoned in the former class though it is as we have seen an anonymous prophecy—Malachi being a designation and not a proper name.

The rest of the titles, fourteen in number, are simply descriptive of the contents of the books, Genesis, Exodus, Leviticus, Numbers, Deuteronomy, Judges, Kings, Chronicles, Psalms, Proverbs, Ecclesiastes, Song of Solomon, Lamentations. Similar in kind with this latter descriptive class is the name " Book of Praises," which is found in the original. We might justly paraphrase it as " Hymn Book," ὕμνος (*hymnos*, " hymn ") being as you know a "song of praise;" and this will agree precisely with what I will presently show as to the book itself, that in the form we have it, it is simply the Hymn Book prepared for the liturgical song of the second Temple. The name we have just mentioned was the oldest name of the collection, and is so recognized by the few Christian writers of the first centuries whose knowledge extended to the Hebrew. We find an allusion to it as early as the second century by Hippolytus of Rome, who may be known to you from Baron Bunsen's very readable book "Hippolytus and his Times" (*Hippolytus und seine zeit*, 2 volumes, 1853). You may not be aware that it is to Bunsen though a foreigner and a diplomate, we are in no small degree indebted for the re-awakening of the critical study of the Old Testament in England, which had almost lain dormant since Castell and the great scholars who co-operated with him in the London Polyglot.

Somewhat later this same name is mentioned as being the original one in the preface of Jerome's revision of the old Latin translation, which is now known to us as the Vulgate, a revision which has shared the fate of almost all critical versions of the Scriptures. In his own age its author was anathematized even by so great an authority as Augustine, as an innovator and disturber of men's minds, only in a later time to be canonized by a grateful church, and to have his version pronounced by the Tridentine Council the ultimate appeal in all matters of faith.

This name, *Tehillim*, or Hymn Book, further possesses among the Jews an unbroken tradition in its favor, so there can remain no reasonable doubt that it is the title which was given this collection by those who first collated and edited it into its present shape.

Our common name, Psalms, comes from the Greek translation to which I have already alluded, as having in one way or another such influence in shaping the nomenclature of our English version.

Ψαλμός (*Psalmos*, Psalm), in Greek means primarily the twanging of a harp or any stringed instrument—then a Song which is sung to such stringed accompaniment, or later to any musical accompaniment, finally means no more than "a piece set to music." In this latter sense it is used to translate the original מִזְמוֹר *mizmor.*—" A Song to be sung to the orchestral accompaniment of the Temple," which we find in the inscription of fifty-seven of these Psalms.

Of the musical arrangements of the Temple service I will speak later, but be good enough to look a moment at the fourth Psalm for the origin of this word. We lose in the English "Psalm of David" the real pith and meaning of the inscription, whose sense

HISTORY OF THE NAME PSALM. 83

is "belonging to David, that is, to the collection of sacred songs called after David's name," a literary note as to the author for the benefit of the reader—the further musical note (*mizmor*), added for the benefit of the Temple-choir, indicates that this composition was to be accompanied in the service by the music of the orchestra; the two notes having no connection, and being probably from different hands—one from the literary, the other from the musical editor of this collection. We should have,—"by David, an orchestral melody." The Greek renders this musical note fairly well by Ψαλμός, *psalmos*.

As it was found in the reading of so large a number of the Songs, (and moreover when the Greek translation was made, this collection had long been used in the musical service of the Temple,) they give to the entire collection the name Ψαλμοί, *psalmoi*, "musical compositions," or "musical collection"—"of the Temple," of course, being understood.

You are doubtless aware that all the Christian writings which are collected in the New Testament were, perhaps with the exception of the Gospel of Matthew and the Epistle to the Hebrews, written for Greek speaking peoples, few if any of whom were conversant with the Hebrew. It is for this reason that the writers when referring to the older Scripture both in their quotations and their nomenclature make use of the Greek translation and not of the original.

The Βίβλος Ψαλμῶν, "Psalm Book" mentioned in Luke xx. 42, Acts i. 20, is the title taken from the Septuagint, and shows that as early as our era this title was the common one in the Greek version for this collection.

So far there could be no misapprehension in the name; to all the Greek speaking peoples the name Psalm carried the meaning of a song set to music. The Book of Psalms was understood as the collection of such songs used in the musical service of the Temple. The confusion arises with the old Latin version, made during the second century in the provincial Latin of North Africa and from imperfect manuscripts of the Greek, but which early gained such hold upon the people of the Latin tongue, that it was only after a long struggle and many anathemas that the later version from the original by Jerome succeeded in replacing it. In the Psalter however this old version had acquired a peculiar sacredness through its constant use in the daily service, and neither the clergy nor people were willing to give up for a new version, however accurate, the old Psalter whose very words and rhythm had grown to be an integral part of their worship.

I cannot here go into the history of the Latin

versions, nor would it be profitable that I should do so. Jerome's translation from the original text in the Psalter did not gain acceptance beyond scholars. The old Latin with all the errors of the Septuagint and a goodly number which must be laid at its own door, continued with slight revisions in the Roman and Gallican Psalter to be the service book of the Roman Church, and at the Reformation was simply translated into the vernacular by those bodies who retained the liturgical forms.

It is to this old Latin version we owe, I can hardly say a debt of gratitude for our word Psalm. If you ever come to compare this old Latin with the Greek, you will find it, in its minute and painful verbalness, betraying not the accuracy but the ignorance of the translators. Whenever they meet with a word which is obscure, they simply transcribe it as best they can with Latin letters. So it is that there has come into the Psalter, both in the inscriptions and the Psalms themselves, a mass of mongrel words belonging to no language under the heaven, that have furnished food for much mystical speculation which might as well have been spared.

Most important of these creations of the old Latin translators is the word *Psalm*. Evidently at a loss for the meaning of the Greek Ψαλμός, they adopted the easy method of transliterating it with Latin letters into Psalmus. Of course, to the Latin peoples, to whom the word had no association, no natural significance, it became emptied of all the meaning, "Song set to music," with the allusion to the Temple service ever borne with it to the Alexandrian Jews. It conveyed no idea extending beyond this collection, or some part of it. In this sense it came into use in ecclesiastical Latin, and with unessential changes of form, has passed into all the languages of Europe, which have come under the influence of the Latin Church. In good English usage the word carries with it no shade of its original meaning nor of its history. It has almost come to be a proper name, designating, in the plural, Psalms, this collection of Hebrew sacred poems—in the singular, Psalm, some one of them; thence in modern English it signifies any song or poem written after the same fashion.

I trust I have made clear to you the history of our name Psalms. 1. It originated in the Greek translation, where it designates the collection as one of "Songs set to music," in a word "Music Book of the Temple." 2. That the name as we now have it, evacuated of all its old meaning, and simply designating, as a proper name, this collection, comes from the Latin of the old Itala. Should we too closely interrogate the history of our nomenclature, in any department, I fear our vocabulary would be small. The name has become fixed in the best technical and popular usage, and as it conveys an intelligible idea, there is no reason for a change. Only bear in mind that the name is not the original one of this collection, and even in the sense in which we now use it in English, it has lost its characteristic meaning.

Another name in common use with us for this collection is "Psalter." As the name Psalm which we have just explained, this also comes from the Greek. Ψαλτήριον (*Psalterium*) is a stringed instrument in regard to which there is some dispute among archæologists as to whether it were over or under-strung, that is, as to whether it were a harp or a lyre. The name seems to have been used metaphorically by the Jews of Alexandria for their Psalm Book, just as the present wont is to call our collections of sacred melodies The Harp, The Lyre, The Trumpet or some similar name. It was probably not given by the Greek translators, but through long popular usage grew to be the generally accepted name of the collection among the Greek speaking communities of the dispersion. It was the Harp which, as they met from Sabbath to Sabbath, afar among the Gentiles, recalled to them the sacred music of their Temple.

The early Latin versions were good borrowers, even if they were nothing else, so this term could not fail them. That they do not understand it is of small moment. They have the Latin alphabet and can transliterate, so the Latin is speedily blessed with a new word, Psalterium, or perhaps I should say a new meaning for an older word, as Psalterium had been borrowed from the Greek as early as the Augustan age, in its original sense of harp.

In ecclesiastical Latin this name came to be the technical term for the Psalm collection as used in the Church service. Thus we have the celebrated Gallican and Roman Psalters, so named from their respective use in the Gallican or Roman Church service, which represent the first unsuccessful attempt of Jerome to improve the text of the old Latin, and to the former of which the Anglican Prayer Book is in no small degree beholden.

From the Latin the name passed in a similar sense into all the modern languages of Europe. In English we find the term most in use by those reformed religious bodies in whose service the reading of the Psalms forms some stated part.

Psalter then is a Greek word—meaning Harp, which becomes first the vulgar, then the generally accepted name of their collection of sacred melodies among the Jews of the Dispersion. Passing into the Latin with the loss of its original meaning, it becomes the technical name of the Psalm collection, as used statedly in the service—a meaning it still largely retains in English.

There are other less important names in use in English to designate this collection, but I cannot pause to speak of them now. You perceive our common names all come from the Greek translation. Should we call the book as its original editors have done, we should be obliged to say, " Praise Book, or Hymn Book."

But let us now turn to the Arrangement of the collection.

The " Book of Psalms" is a collection of religious poems from all ages and styles of Hebrew literature, which have been critically and metrically edited for use in the service of song of the Second Temple.

None of the early literature of the Hebrew people which has come down to us is so varied in character, none bears such traces of editorial emendation and arrangement as does this collection.

Let me ask you to examine with me,

I. *Its Literary*, and II. *Its Liturgical Arrangement.*

The Psalms, as we now have them, are divided into Five Books, which are clearly distinguished from one another in the original by appropriate spacing and by the names, Second, Third, Fourth and Fifth Books before each of the succeeding sections.

The only traces we have of these books in the English version are the closing formulæ or doxologies at the end of each section, which are lost to the ordinary reader by their being attached as a final verse to the preceding Psalm.

The first book is 'from Psalm ii. to Psalm xli., with the closing formula, Psalm xli. 13.

The second book, Psalms xlii—lxxii., the formula Psalm lxxii. 18, 19,—on the twentieth verse I will speak in a moment.

The third book, Psalms lxxiii—lxxxix.—final formula, Psalm lxxxix. 52.

The fourth book, Psalms xc–cvi., formula Psalm cvi. 48.

The fifth book, Psalms cvii.–cxlix.; as a closing formula, we may regard Psalm cl. which became a sort of epilogue to the entire collection when this fifth and final book was added to it.

What we call the first Psalm was also added in the final making up of the collection as an introduction or prologue, and does not in the early time seem to have been counted in the number of the Psalms. If you will turn to Acts xiii. 33 you will find in our English version Psalm ii. 7 quoted from the second Psalm, but we are able to say on manuscript authority (for which see Tischendorf's eighth edition) that it was quoted in the original hand as from the first Psalm. Some later reader finding the quotation in what in his Psalter had become the second Psalm, corrects what he supposes was the oversight of the original writer, by setting second in the place of first. From this later hand it is that *second* in this passage has come into the received Greek text, and thence by translation into the English. We can see now how the writer of the Acts could with perfect accuracy have quoted this passage as in the first Psalm, and have a striking illustration of the little learning which has done so much to improve and destroy for us nearly all the literary remains of antiquity.

The number of Psalms in our version is one hundred and fifty—merely an accidental agreement with the later form of the original. One hundred and fifty is not, as many suppose, either the sacred or constant number of the Psalms. The number at an earlier time more common in the original was one hundred and forty-seven gained from the same material by a somewhat dissimilar arrangement. It is this number that the Hagadic exegesis of the Talmud—an exegesis whose highest flight was to make acrostic— has in view when it compares the Psalms to the years of Jacob. We know, moreover, that in the Hebrew manuscripts of a different school from those on which our printed text is based the number is one hundred and forty-nine. Though the Septuagint has also one hundred and fifty Psalms, they are arranged either by union or separation of several of the poems in a way materially different from that in our version

—it unites into one, Psalms ix., x., and Psalms cxiv., cxv., and divides into two, Psalm cxvi. (verses 1-9 and 10-19), and Psalm cxlvii. (verses 1-11 and 12-20). In this arrangement of the Greek the Vulgate has followed, and it remains the common usage of the Latin Church.

The Greek translators add to their collection an apocryphal Psalm, known as the hundred and fifty-first, which the later Syriac, Arabic and Ethiopic versions copy from them. It pretends to be the thanksgiving of David on his victory over Goliath, and I had thought of reading it to you. However, I will not occupy your time with it. It is simply of no value, and bears on its face such clear marks of manufacture that even Ptolemy's scholars who drew into their canon all accessible Hebrew Literature, whether good or bad, have to state in a note their disbelief in its genuineness.

As regards the number and arrangement of the Psalms in our English version, though this agrees in the main with the printed editions of the Hebrew, it seems to the best scholars probable that in several instances for textual and internal reasons it would be difficult to make clear to you, it should be slightly changed. If ever you have an old oriental manuscript in your hands, and notice how with but the slightest spacing, without number and without other outward indication, the sections of a book or the cantos of a poem are divided, you can understand how without design or conscious intent, but simply through the haste or carelessness of copyists, there has often come into the later manuscripts an arrangement in many respects dissimilar from that of the original. It is a phenomenon found in all literature, which has come to us in a written state, and there is no reason why Hebrew literature should be exempted from it.

'One of the most important tasks of the science known to us as "textual criticism," is to determine from internal evidence whether the arrangement of the matter, as we find it in the late manuscripts which have come to us, is that of the original authors or editors. This kind of criticism, applied to the text of the Psalms, leads us to believe that the arrangement of our English version, in one or two cases, differs from that of the original editors. It seems probable that originally a few Psalms, which are now separated, formed but one poem, namely:

Psalms ix., x., both parts of one long, alphabetic poem and correctly united in the Greek.

Psalms xlii., xliii., shown to be but one Psalm by their common style and rhythm, and so found in our best manuscripts.

Psalm cxvii., with its two verses, seems to be

merely the opening verses of the following Psalm, cxviii., or the close of the preceding Psalm, cxvi.

The further union of Psalms cxiii., cxiv., and Psalms cxxxiv., cxxxv., which not a few scholars have approved, does not seem to me to rest on either internal or manuscript grounds of sufficient weight.

It seems probable that there are united as one Psalm in our version, poems which were originally separate, namely:

Psalm xxiv., one poem, verses 1–6; a new and entirely different one, verses 7–10.

Psalm xxvii., first poem, verses 1–6; second poem, verses 7–14.

Psalm xxxii., first poem, verses 1–7; second poem, verses 8–11.

Psalm xix., is also regarded by many as composed of two separate poems.

That each of the three Psalms, xxiv., xxvii., xxxii., is composed of two poems, is clear to any one who has sufficient acquaintance with the original to appreciate the evidence of literary form and style. It is not clear, however, and this is the point I wish to make, that their combination is due to the error of copyists; it is rather the work of the first editors, who combined them for liturgical reasons I shall hereafter make plain to you.

Our arrangement then agrees in the main with

what we have reason to believe was the original one. The only changes we can make in our version with reasonable surety are the combination into one Psalm of Psalms ix., and x., xlii., and xliii., cxvi., and cxvii., leaving, you perceive, one hundred and forty-seven Psalms, just the number mentioned as the old one in the Talmudic legend spoken of above.

We are told in the Midrash[1] to Psalm iii., that when Rabbi Joshua Ben Levi was beginning some investigations into the authorship of the Psalms, he was arrested at the very outset by a voice from Heaven saying to him, "Wake not those who have fallen asleep—disturb not the grave of our king David." It is a voice which has not reached modern scholars, for no book of antiquity has been submitted to such minute and constant investigation.

The result of these investigations in respect to our next point, the collection of these poems into their present shape, is very clear, and on all the essential points practically unanimous.

Please remember the object for which this collection was made, to furnish a hymn-book for the service of the Second Temple, and you will have a clue to help you in our investigation. It was not designed as an anthology from their best poems, nor was it com-

[1] A Midrash is an old Jewish exposition or commentary, usually full of anecdote. (T.)

menced and carried through with any purely literary motive. The first and sole object of its editors was to compile from the religious poetry of their nation a collection of sacred songs for the worship of the Temple.

We saw in the last hour that the shape in which we have the Hebrew literature is post-exilic, *i. e.*, it is the result of the movement then inaugurated to place their sacred literature, much of which had been scattered or destroyed through the Assyrian invasions, in some more permanent and compendious form, which would be safe amid the new dangers which environed and threatened to obliterate it.

One of the first of these collections would be of religious songs for their re-established Temple worship. Here the compilers would not be obliged to make an original collection—they needed simply to draw on the old "Hymn Books" of the former Temple. That such existed we should *a priori* be led to suppose from the necessities of the musical service of the former Temple, as to which we shall presently speak. Not only this, but we have preserved in Psalm lxxii., 20, the very name of the principal source which our present editors have made use of in forming their collection, the תְּפִלּוֹת דָּוִד *Tephilloth David,* "The Prayers of David," the verse here being the closing formula of the old roll containing this Davidic collection, which the new editors with the unthinking accuracy so characteristic of the Shemitic mind, have taken into their collection with the poem which immediately preceded it. That these "Prayers of David" can not refer to the previous Psalms or Psalm Book scarcely needs the saying, as many of these are referred to other authors (xlii.–xlix.–l.) It is of a kind with the subscription we find, Jeremiah li., 64; Job xxxi., 40.

The name translated here "Prayer" means rather "Devotional Hymn," "Sacred Hymn." It is found in the original as the inscription of Psalms xvii., lxxxvi., xc., cii., cxlii., also in Habakkuk iii., 1, and in Hannah's triumphant Magnificat, 1 Samuel ii.

Many scholars suppose that these "Sacred Hymns of David" were an old Temple-collection begun by David, to whom the organization of the religious music is very constantly referred, and which to a large degree, though not exclusively, was composed of his own melodies. Whenever we have an inscription in our version stating that the Psalm is "of David" it is almost invariably a mistranslation of the original.

The original לְדָוִד (literally "to David") is a note made by the compilers having the simple meaning that the poem in question either was taken by them from this Davidic collection or supposed by them to belong to it—this notice of course giving no judgment as to whether any particular Psalm be of

David's own personal composition or not, merely stating it belonged to the collection which bore his name, and leaving open to us to decide from the internal evidence of the poem itself, and such outside allusion as may be accessible, whether it be his or not. I am aware that this view can not be found in the commentaries, while our lexicons give a force to the much discussed Hebrew particle which they have borrowed from their knowledge of its translation in the modern versions. I am convinced however on a careful investigation of the textual phenomena of the Psalms that it is the only theory that can enable us, with any regard to the results of linguistic and critical study, to retain our respect for the old tradition as to their origin, preserved to us in the editorial inscriptions. The English translation "of David" "by David," is not only incorrect in itself, but also misleading, as the theories built upon it satisfactorily attest.

I say the note as to the authorship is clearly of editorial origin. Take any modern Hymn Book, and from whom is the foot or head-note as to the author of the hymn or tune? Clearly from the compiler or editor of the collection, who, if he be accurate and painstaking, endeavors to gather information as to the age and authorship of the hymns in his collection from all sources he deems trustworthy. It would seem a fact too patent to need proof that Wesley or Watts did not write over each of their hymns "by Charles Wesley," or "by Isaac Watts." When we find such an inscription in any hymn book of to-day, no one for a moment supposes that it has been copied from the manuscript of the author, but it is universally recognized as a note by the editor for the information of his reader. And yet a theory precisely like this has been held by many scholars as to the Psalms, that David, or the other singers when they wrote a poem, wrote over it "by David" and the like, and the later editors have simply transcribed with the poem this also, and so it must have equal authority with the poem itself, and must be regarded as a sure clue to the authorship of the Psalm.

If you are at all conversant with the literature of the Psalms, you will know with what hot words the question of the authority and origin of these inscriptions has been debated, and what seas of ink have been shed in settling it. Perhaps I may now, as well as later, sum up the controversy in a few words.

The Jewish schoolmen and doctors were too busy in the early time with their questions of liturgy and ethics, which they have embodied for us in the Talmud, to produce any rational or critical exegesis. The Midrash, perverting the truth which lies hid in their old tradition that God has revealed His Law in seventy-two languages, *i. e.*, has given it a new force and meaning to each people to whom it comes, endeavored to read as many interpretations as possible into the word of Scripture, and so degenerated into a system of conceits or allegorizing. When the Talmud had been completed and they came to study and explain the Scripture, it was to count its letters and invent a subtle system of signs to mark their quantity. Do you ask bread of the Jewish schoolmen, they give you a stone, for in the very things in which they had all the tradition, all the knowledge, and might have been the world's teachers, they have left it in ignorance. But no one dares bring a railing accusation against their scholarship. They were, through the mediæval time, when not only their books but their bodies lit the fires of bigotry and hypocrisy, in their purity of life, their good citizenship, and their thrift, the very leaven of society. It is alone the result of the environments into which they had been forced by misfortune that their exposition of their own writings has remained so meagre and of so small value.

Scholars in these later times have been obliged to lay anew the foundations for the study of their national literature, which they themselves were unable to lay broad and deep enough.

They evidently did not understand these inscriptions, and often treat them as the Muhammedan theologians do the not dissimilar inscriptions to the Surahs of the Koran, as unrevealed mysteries into which it is unlawful to look.

Few Christian scholars of the early time knew the Psalms, save through the Greek and Latin versions, by whose transliteration, rather than translation, the sense of the inscription was rendered unintelligible. Text and notes were not distinguished by them, and they read to a people even more ignorant than themselves the names of tunes and directions to the Temple orchestra as though they were part of the inspired Scripture. It was alone the acute mind of Theodore of Mopsuestia (A. D. 429), most original among the Church Fathers, condemned as a heretic by the party of the ins because he happened to be of the party of the outs, who seemed to have divined the real difference of these inscriptions and notes, but his was the only voice in a thousand years.

The scholars of the Protestant Reformation, which was the return to the authority of an infallible Scripture from the authority of an infallible Church, had tasks of establishing the doctrine of Scripture more essential than questions as to its text.

With the increasing study of the text of Scripture, and the comparison of its versions, together with the growing knowledge of the other oriental languages and their literary usage, these mysterious inscriptions were gradually unravelled. As it became apparent that they were musical and literary notes, it also became apparent that they were no part of the inspired text of Scripture, but mere remarks added to give information to the reader or facilitate the use of the collection in the Temple service. Among the first to announce this view was Richard Simon, a priest of the Oratory at Paris, but he was met by a storm of opposition which has not yet altogether ceased. Biblical scholarship here, as too often elsewhere, forgetting that any inspiration must inhere in the message and not in its literary form, took stand on ground where it has had to make a losing fight, in which many who would fain have wished it well, could not join.

The literature of this inscription discussion on one side or another, is a very large, and, I might add, profitless one.

There are, probably, at the present day, no scholars whose opinion carries weight, who recognize in these inscriptions more than an editorial origin and an editorial authority. Some of the grounds that have led them to reach this view are the following:

I. That it is contrary to all we know of Shemitic style for the author to add notes or inscriptions such as these to his poems or works, of course a technical argument of weight to those alone who can appreciate such style.

II. That in the early time they were regarded so clearly as editorial, that there was little scruple in either changing them or omitting them altogether, when the later scribe or translator imagined he had better information as to the authorship of any Psalm.

The manuscripts of the Hebrew are far from agreeing in them, but even still better illustrative of their lack of authority is their form in the Septuagint. This old Greek version gives an inscription of authorship of some kind to every Psalm, even the late Hallelujah Psalms; ascribes to David some thirteen or fourteen which the Hebrew does not, and drops his name from several ascribed to him in the original. It gives a number of historical data in addition to or at variance with those of the Hebrew text. Some of the Psalms, which in the Hebrew are inscriptionless, it ascribes, without any reason, to Jeremiah or one of the later prophets. Of so little importance do they seem, that some of the versions made from the Greek omit them altogether, from reasons of convenience.

Do you turn to the Targum, or early Jewish paraphrase, you find many of these inscriptions different, not only from the original, but from the almost contemporaneous translation into the Greek. In a word, their varying form, in all the early versions, evinces that they were regarded as no part of the inspired text.

That any modern scholars should have claimed for

them more than editorial value is simply one of the unaccountable whims of scholarship. It has never occurred to any Christian scholar to lay any stress or make any claim for the inscriptions or subscriptions of the New Testament books, which *a priori* one would imagine of more value than those of the Psalms.

These inscriptions or notes added by the editors of our collection are of two kinds :

(1.) Giving information as to the author of the Psalm with any circumstances accompanying or occasioning its composition, but more frequently, merely the name of the collection from which it had been borrowed. When the author of the Psalm was not known, or, as some of the later Psalms, (as cviii., made up from lvii. and lx.), it is simply a cento from older poems arranged for the liturgical worship, it has no inscription.

(2.) Even more numerous than these literary notes are the musical ones, found, not only in the inscriptions, but in the body of the text, סֶלָה *Selah*, for example. These give us the tune to which the songs are set, the instrument upon which they are to be performed, with various minute instructions for the proper tone and time to the Temple choir and orchestra. These we will take up when we come hereafter to speak of the musical editing of the Psalms.

The literary notes I will strive to make clear to

you, as we now consider the growth and arrangement of the several books, through whose final collection into one our present Psalter is made up. We must bear in mind, then, that these inscriptions are no more than annotations by the collectors, and our idea of their authority in determining beyond dispute the authorship and age of a Psalm, is to be determined by our judgment of the authority inhering in these collectors. One school insists they must in every case be regarded as of last resort; another that they have no value, but are merely marginal annotations of later readers which have by mistake crept into the text, and so should have no influence upon our independent opinion gained from personal study and analysis of the Psalm.

The wiser view is that they give us the earliest information we have as to the origin and authorship of these poems and are therefore of priceless historical value; that we should regard them of the same authority that we do the annotations of any hymn collector of the present time, who has in his hands the best original material and has evinced himself skilful, painstaking and trustworthy in its use. We accept his annotations as correct in all cases where there are not convincing internal or external reasons which force us to believe that in this or that particular case he has been mistaken.

Just so the literary inscriptions of the Psalms are to be regarded as correct and trustworthy guides to the authorship of the poems, save in the case of some one or other particular Psalm, where there are internal reasons either of literary form or allusion to events, which we are able to fix from contemporaneous history, compelling us to believe that the editor must have been misinformed or mistaken. This may seem a long discussion of a small matter, but it is one on which have hinged all the manifold opinions which have prevailed as to the Psalms.

I have already pointed out the division of the Psalms into five books. These were not collected simultaneously, but separately, by different hands and at longer or shorter intervals, during a period which has been variously estimated, but probably cannot exceed two centuries. All these separate collections, or the best part of each, were then finally combined into one general and received "Hymn Collection" for the Temple service, which ever thereafter continued to be the one in common use.

We shall first examine the collection of each separate book, and then their union into one larger collection.

Book I. includes Psalms ii.–xli., with the closing formula xli., 13. Psalm i., does not belong to this book, but was first added as a prologue to the entire collection, when later this was formed from these five older hymn books. We saw that the writer of the Acts did not count it among the Psalms.

This book, as is attested both by its position and the general style of its poetry, is the oldest of the five books. It was probably formed immediately upon the reëstablishment of the worship after the return from the Exile. It is composed of forty hymns, which are not, however, an original collection of the editors, but were taken by them entirely from the earlier præ-exilic book, "The Devotional Songs of David,"— perhaps a selection from its more familiar melodies. That it was thus collected is indicated by the note as to the authorship, לְדָוִד " to David," found before all the poems save three—ii., x., xxxiii.

Psalm x., as we have seen, was at a late date separated from Psalm ix., through the carelessness of copyists, and so is, in reality, part of the preceding Psalm.

There is reason to believe that the inscription of Psalm xxxiii. has fallen out, though it is possible that it is anonymous.

Psalm ii. is the only one in the first book where an inscription clearly seems to have been originally lacking. This Psalm may be considered either as an introductory Psalm to this single book as Psalm i. is to the entire collection, or as a favorite melody of the old worship, which did not belong to the Davidic collection, and whose author is unknown. By whom and when it was written, as we have no hint from either history or tradition, we are obliged to decide upon the internal evidence of style and situation.

It may be said once for all in regard to the thirty-four " widowed or bereaved " (יְתוֹמִים) *i. e.*, inscriptionless Psalms, that the only grounds for any decision as to the authorship are of necessity internal. The early editors gave no inscriptions because they were not clear as to them. The inscriptions found with them in the early versions vary so greatly among themselves, that they but further confirm us in the belief that there was no sure tradition in regard to them in the early time.

When we examine Psalm ii., it appears that it cannot have been written by any King of Israel, such as David was, for it is addressed *to* some King of Israel by one of his people. The situation is besides apparently non-Davidic. Delitzsch, perhaps the most conservative expositor of the Psalms, who can lay any claim to oriental scholarship, refers it to the Assyrian (the heathen of the first verse) invasions during the reign of Hezekiah. Were we to read the Psalm together, as I had at one time proposed, I am convinced you would find that this is the position in Jewish history which most strikingly illustrates it. But this is the earliest period which can, with reasonable fairness, be assumed for it. The opinions as to its date among scholars have ranged through the next seven centuries. It has been referred to the inroads of the Scythian hordes—to the Chaldean invasion, which ended in the overthrow of the Jewish state—to the dangers which environed the colony of returned Exiles, while rebuilding their city and Temple—to the vexatious oppressions of the Persian General Bageses—to the siege of Jerusalem by Ptolemy Lagi—to the miseries of the people during the dynastic strife between the Ptolemies and the Seleucidæ—to the dangers threatened from the Samaritans, under the High Priest Onias—to the persecutions of Antiochus Epiphanes.

LECTURE IV.

WE proceed to-day with our lectures on the Psalms from the point at which we were obliged to leave off with the closing of the last hour.

I then endeavored to make clear to you that the original name of our Psalm collection was Praise Book or Hymn Book, so called because it was a collection of religious songs made for the worship of the Temple, and that our English names Psalms and Psalter came to us from the early Latin translations of the Septuagint, in a sense quite different from that in which they were used in the Greek.

Taking up the arrangement of the Psalter, I showed you the five books into which it was divided, and, after discussing at some length the question of the inscriptions, arrived at the conclusion that neither of the extreme views in regard to them was, on literary ground, tenable—that their origin was demonstrably editorial and chiefly of historical value.

We then began our survey of the separate Psalms, and had proceeded no farther than the Second Psalm. As the last word in closing, I mentioned that not a few scholars had referred its composition to the reign of Alexander Jannæus, B. C. 105-79, a period which, despite the ever recurring internal disorder and foreign invasion, was one of literary activity, and from which we have preserved to us the Apocryphal books of Judith and Tobit.

This last view was on the point of leading me to call your attention to an interesting question in the critical study of the Psalms, still under discussion, and yet very far from any satisfactory settlement, which we will now take up.

It is a view which seems to have forced itself upon many scholars, even as long ago as Esrom Rudinger, (who was professor for a time in Wittenberg, a colleague there of Melancthon, and who died in 1591,) that the historical situation and allusions in some of the Psalms can only be explained by their authorship in the Maccabean times. Despite Ewald's assertion, made with his customary bitterness and haste, that the very inclining toward this view argues such blunting of the moral and critical judgment as to render one incapable of justly weighing the evidence at issue, the great majority of Shemitic scholars who have been capable of weighing the evidence, do, at the present day, in one form or another, hold this view.

Justus Olshausen, formerly Professor in Kiel, and now Chief Secretary of the Prussian Ministry of Education, in his Commentary on the Psalms, which for textual and grammatical study is, beyond dispute, the most valuable we have, takes the ground which to most of you will doubtless be startling, that the old songs of the Temple worship were all displaced in the Maccabean times by a new collection of religious and patriotic songs, which had sprung from the inspiration of that period of national and intellectual revival— that, at the utmost, not more than half a dozen Psalms, ii., xx., xxi., xxviii., lxi., lxiii., which contain too clear allusions to a Jewish kingdom to be explained away, can possibly have come from præ-exilic times. It is this Maccabean collection, he endeavors to prove, on many grounds that seem to him of great weight, which we have in our Book of Psalms. I do not call your attention to this view for the sake of its novelty. Were it the vagary of an erratic scholar, I should not have mentioned it, but as the carefully elaborated theory of a master in the front rank of his profession, in which the study and reflection of years have only confirmed him, it demands our consideration. With the sharpness of definition, which Olshausen gives to his theory, there are probably few who hold it.

In the modified form, that the last three books of the Psalter are Maccabean in origin, it is held by a considerable number, and thence through all grades of belief or disbelief, until we reach the four Psalms xliv., lxxiv., lxxix., lxxxiii., which, fairness compels me to say, are regarded as undoubtedly of Maccabean origin by many of the best authorities of the present day. I think myself that the authorities may be in error here, but before I can tell you why, we must see clearly just what the Maccabean era is. The discussion of it will be of further value in fixing for us the period from which came the latest songs of our collection.

Antiochus the Fourth, known in history by the name Epiphanes, the Illustrious, given him by his flatterers, was the son of Antiochus the Great. His fame has come down to us through the Jewish Apocrypha as a bloody and ferocious tyrant; through Diodorus and the Greek historians as an eccentric voluptuary. And yet it seems to me that neither the one or the other fairly gauges the character of Epiphanes—that he is one of the little understood and misjudged characters of history. Like Diocletian he was a man by natural bent liberal in mind and kindly in disposition, whom political circumstances beyond his control forced to assume unwillingly the rôle of a persecutor. Educated in Rome, he was through an intrigue which ended in the poisoning of his brother, brought to the throne of Syria while still a young man. He inherited from his house their military traditions and boundless ambition. Conscious of his ability to play a wider part than that of mere viceroy of Syria, and holding in his hand sufficient force to at last crush out his hated rivals, the Ptolemies, his hopes were dashed, and his plans, just ready to mature, were blighted by the interference of the Romans, who reduced him to a vassal. His disappointed ambition beat its wings against the narrow bounds of his own territory; his failure embittered him and prepared him to wreak on the Jews, when later they opposed him, the indignities to which he himself had been exposed. He was beside a visionary. When all hope of increasing his territory by arms had passed away, he endeavored to bring together the diverse nationalities and religions under his sway, through some one cultus which might become a common bond of union to all his people. There seems to have been in his mind some dim prefigurement of that coincident church and state which became the ideal of the mediæval ages. Least of all did he expect resistance from the Jews. He was surrounded by Jewish parasites who assured him their people were eager for a change, and he could gain small reverence for a religion, the candidates for

whose most sacred office—the High Priesthood—
bargained and wrangled at his doors over the price of
their investiture. There were very many among the
Jews themselves, who looked upon his first innovations with undisguised sympathy and favor—their
cultured and monied class had long since been
Hellenized. He built a gymnasium in Jerusalem
which became a centre for the Greek learning and the
Greek games. On his first return from Egypt, he
entered an illuminated city amid the acclamations of
the inhabitants. He should not bear the blame of
misinterpreting a popular sentiment which seemed so
favorable to him. It was but the natural outgrowth
of his theocratic policy for him to set up in the Temple
at Jerusalem some symbol of the national cultus on
the Altar of Jehovah, who, education taught him,
was a mere local divinity though one to whom his
belief and disposition led him to show tolerance and
respect. The placing of the Eagle of Zeus as a
tutelar divinity on the Altar of Burnt Offering was
accompanied by riots in Jerusalem, which the Hellenized Jews of his Court assured him were the results of
political sedition. He sends an army to enforce
order, which is met by open defiance. In a moment
of despairing passion at seeing what were his fondest
dreams for the union and well-being of his people
miscarry, he gives orders to crush out with fire and

sword, all opposition to his commands. Once more he is advised by the apostate Jews of his court that the only way to crush the sedition is by crushing the distinctive religion which was its rallying point, so he committed the folly of his life by inhibiting, under pain of death, the worship and customs they held most sacred. He matched his armies against the moral and religious force of the Jews, and to such a conflict, as history has often shown, there could be but one result. Justice to his memory should compel even his enemies to admit that he himself did not take part in the persecution; he left it to his generals and to renegades, who in all ages have been the most willing instruments for persecuting the faith they once professed. Starting on an expedition to Persia to replenish his impoverished exchequer, he fails in this too, and dies on his homeward way, February, 164, B. C., a broken and disappointed man, all whose schemes for the aggrandizement of his state and welfare of his subjects have been misunderstood and have failed. He can only leave to his nine years old son a heritage of disorder, war and speedy murder.

I have thus sketched to you the character of Epiphanes, because I conceive that history has done him injustice. He was not a great man even as the world estimates greatness. With the ambition of an Alexander, and the theocratic ideal of a Leo, he was confined to a narrow stage where his every plan was thwarted. He is chiefly known to the after time by his persecution of the Jews, which resulted in their revolt, and ushered in a period of their history of which they may justly be proud,—the Maccabean Era.

Had Epiphanes confined himself to his first Greek innovations, the Hellenizing element of the Jewish people would probably have been strong enough to hold the Puritan party in check. It was not until, when maddened by the first show of resistance he strove to crush out the religion of Israel, that all parties became united into one. The blood of the first martyrs cemented together all elements of the people into a common resistance. A priest in an obscure village slays an officer of the royal dragonnade, flies to the desert with his sons, and becomes there the nucleus of a religious and military awakening of the Jewish people without parallel in their previous or subsequent history. Driven asunder again and again by the royal troops, it is only to rally in gathering force.

It was a conflict, not for aggrandizement, not even for national existence, for all hope of either had long ago faded away; it was a struggle for the toleration of their religion and the right to worship Jehovah.

Rarely have a people fought with such noble devotion for their faith, even when their arms have been steeled by this holiest passion of which men are capable. Under the lead of Judas the Maccabi—the Hammerer, *i. e.*, the one through whom God beats down his enemies, they defeat, after varying fortunes, the Syrian forces who more than thrice outnumber them, restore the worship of Jehovah to His Temple, and compel a religious toleration.

The furnace of persecution through which they had passed, had purified the people from its worthless elements, and with the restoration of their worship, came a revival of religious devotion such as they had never known before. Of their political and military success, it is not in place to speak here, but it was evanescent. Within a few years it was marred by an intolerance and corruption which confirm clearly the lesson of all history, that no hands are so unfit to hold the sceptre of government as those of a priest.

The religious reformation and revival were alone of enduring influence, and cast the Jewish character into a mould, which it has since then, to a large degree, maintained. In modern history we have no period parallel to it. In some small degree we may compare it with the resistance of the Scotch Kirk to the Anglican Prelacy, or the struggles of the Waldensians against the interdict of Pope Lucius III.

It is periods of persecution such as this which always produce the most tender and delicate religious poetry among every people. An examination of our choicest hymns will show this to the satisfaction of any of you. Now, say the scholars who hold the theory of Maccabean Psalms, it would be a fact no less than remarkable if a religious revolution, so far-reaching in its influence, had left no trace of itself in the religious songs of the Temple worship.

A priori, there can be no objection to this theory, either first, on religious grounds, for no period of Jewish history shows so pure a religious fervor as does this. If Jehovah ever dwelt among His people, and inspired His servants, it was at this time, when they were, with small hope of success, exposing themselves to the death for His worship. There are few of the prophets or saints of the older time who can compare in religious devotion or moral force with the men of this age. The writer of the Hebrews sees this well in borrowing from this period many of his figures of the men of faith of whom the world was not worthy.

Nor second, can there be any objection on canonical ground. Despite all positive assertions pro and contra, we simply do not know when the canon was closed, that is, when the books came into their present shape, nor can I see any interest save a purely historical one in the inquiry. We only know that at a much later time men were still discussing the canonicity of several or all the writings. It is the decision of this question, as to whether these are Maccabean Psalms or not, which forms one of the chief factors in our subsequent decision as to the time when the canon was closed. Of course you well know that neither in mathematics or literature can one unknown quantity be used to solve another. But even granting the canon was closed, there can be no possible objection to the view of many of the more conservative scholars that several hymns of this period, which had grown sacred to the people, were added either on the margin, or at the end of the rolls for use in worship, and finally, by the hand of later copyists came into the body of the text. The view of the New Testament text, which guides the scholars now preparing our new English version, is that there may be, and are, additions (for instance, the narrative in John vii. 53–viii. 11,) which have come into the text at a later time. I am unable to see why the same course of criticism is not applicable to the Hebrew text.

Nor lastly, is the linguistic ground, which has been urged by many, of any weight. Doubtless the Hebrew had, in a large measure, ceased to be a spoken language ere the period of the Maccabees, but it was still the language of the Temple service and of scholars. As little as does the beautiful Latinity of the hymns of Thomas of Celano (1255) or Bernard of Clairvaux (1153) prove that the Latin must, in their time, have been a spoken dialect, does the purity of the Hebrew in any Psalm prove, beyond necessity of further discussion, that it could not have been written in the Maccabean era.

We have, then, you perceive, no inherent impossibility of such Psalms; let us now inquire what the real facts in the case are.

And first, the theory of Olshausen is, without hesitation, on every literary and linguistic ground to be rejected. Olshausen belongs to a school of criticism to whom tradition is of no value, and who use history only as a means of confirming their own subjective judgments as to how things ought to have been. In Biblical criticism this school has received, by way of disapprobation I suppose, the name German, but we must not give our neighbors unjustly a bad name. It had its origin in England in the seventeenth century, and not until a much later day does it pass through France to Germany. Its hasty judgments, and unproven theories, have been the reason why, in this country, the legitimate critical study of the Bible, even by those who cherish its accredited and ascertained teachings as a guide of life, and who have no end in view save by their studies the better to understand it, has fallen into such disrepute. Olshausen's theory involves literary difficulties twice as insuperable as those from which he endeavors to escape. It gives the lie to all the traditions which the editors of the Psalm collection have embodied in the inscriptions, and necessitates a reshaping of all Jewish history, which of course is no difficulty to one who believes that there was no Jewish literature prior to the eighth century. There is no limit to the credulity of those who assume that there is no truth in history.

On literary ground it is inconceivable how the old religious melodies should have so irrecoverably perished. A religious revival such as the Maccabean would only fix them the firmer in the affections of the people.

If they are Maccabean in origin, how is it that this same collection is found in the translation of the Septuagint, contemporaneous at the latest with the Maccabean period, and made by Greek scholars who if not hostile, were at least indifferent to the Maccabean struggle, and would have taken as the old Temple melodies no collection of Maccabean hymns, and whose ascriptions of the Psalms, in the titles, to the early prophets, show that they were not consciously translating any contemporaneous songs.?

In fact so strong is the argument here that if pressed home on all its lines, it would even show that the

Greek version was made prior to the Maccabean period. Of course, if this be so, it is all over with the Maccabean Psalm collection.

How is it that, not fifty years after this Maccabean struggle, when its memories were still fresh in men's minds, this collection is constantly spoken of as by David and the men of the older time, without any trace of reference to the persecution whose scars had not yet been healed?

Lastly, if we accept as the date of Chronicles the pontificate of the High Priest Jochanan, toward the close of the Persian period, B. C. 405–359, where it is most generally referred, we shall have convincing internal proof against the Maccabean origin of our book, for in 1 Chronicles xvi. 36 we find a cento made up of fragments from Psalms xcvi., cv., cvi., with certain liturgical notes which could not very well have been borrowed until the collection had assumed its present shape.

In a word, could we believe the Psalm Book to be a collection of Maccabean poems, we should have to resign all confidence in history which was not coincident with our own personal experience. Thus you see how a wise investigation of Scripture in many cases but confirms what on other grounds we had been led to have faith in. There is and can be no conflict between scholarship and anything which is really divine in Scripture. The province of literary scholarship is to investigate the literary forms which Scripture has assumed. It must, by its very terms, treat the Hebrew literature as a part of the world's literature. Nothing of permanent value can be touched or destroyed by it. We thus gain for the Hebrew Scripture rational value for all time, which is infinitely more precious than any which is the result of unthinking preconception.

The arguments we have adduced above will be valid as against all the more radical theories of the Maccabean Psalms which are now so commonly held. It is not so clear that there are not three or four Psalms which have in some way come into our collection from this Maccabean revival.

The Psalms which seemingly bear clearest traces of this revival are Psalms lxxiv. and lxxix. I can not pause now to go into a minute exegesis of them, but, to a candid mind, there are many allusions apparently only explicable from the situation of a people persecuted for their religion by heathen enemies, with their Temple the seat of a foreign cultus, and their synagogues all burned, such as we know existed in the Maccabean time, and such as we do not know existed at any other. By some they have been referred very unfitly to the period of the Chaldean invasion, but this had immediately no religious end in view, nor was, in any sense of the word, a persecution; it was a piece of political and military strategy to break the defensive power of Egypt by removing from its boundary a people who were naturally friendly to it. I am inclined myself to leave the question of these two Psalms, as John Calvin did, an open one and for the present undecided. There is a possibility that these two poems are from the Maccabean period; if so, they came into the collection at a later time from the margin or the appendix of the roll. On the other hand, the Greek translation, which contains these same Psalms, creates so strong a case against their Maccabean origin that we are obliged to leave the decision open.

I have dwelt thus long upon this question because it is one of the most widely discussed and important ones in Hebrew literature. If you ever take up the minute study of the Bible, you will find three main and essential points of controversy between scholars in the Old Testament Scriptures—the origin of the Mosaic literature—the authorship of the last twenty-seven chapters of Isaiah,—and this question as to the Maccabean Psalms. We have endeavored to show in regard to it, that, while there is no *a priori* ground against such Psalms, and that the Maccabean era was one in every way fitted to inspire the highest religious poetry, there are overwhelming literary and historical grounds for rejecting any such origin either of the collection or any considerable part of it; it remaining just possible that one or two Psalms from this period, may, through their constant use in the worship, have come into the Temple Hymn Book in the later form in which we have it preserved to us.

Thus we can fix the hither terminus of our Psalm-collection, and we reject without further question the Maccabean origin of Psalm ii., and the other Psalms which is being pushed with such vigor by the newest and most learned school of Hebrew philology. The collection existed substantially in its present shape before the translation of the Septuagint.

We said that the Psalms of this first book, with the exceptions I have mentioned (ii., x., xxxiii.,) all belong to the older Davidic collection; the further question now arises as to how many of them may with justice be referred to David himself. That the inscription "of David" in the English does not necessarily imply personal Davidic authorship, but merely that the Psalm is taken from the older Davidic collection, I have already endeavored to make clear, and will not now revert to it. That a book in the orient is named after the one whose works stand first, or form the most considerable part in it, I might have further illustrated from the Ethiopic Psalter, which is simply known as "David," and the similar usage of the old oriental Greek church; we will read "David, etc."[1]

There are two diametrically opposite views as to the Davidic Psalms, both of which I presume we shall, without discussion, be prepared to pronounce untenable.

I. That David wrote all the Psalms.

We are told in the Talmud that David either wrote in person all the Psalms, or, when other names are mentioned, they are simply those through whom his inspirations have assumed the form in which we now have them. A similar view was held by many of the Church Fathers, as Augustine and Chrysostom, while we find the same in Beda, earliest and far from least of our English scholars. At the present day, it is held by some few scholars of the Latin Church. In the Protestant Church it has been alone defended with more heat than wisdom by a certain Dr. Ludwig Clauss of Berlin, in a book published in 1831. No one of course who accepts even the editorial accuracy of the inscriptions ascribing the Psalms to so many other authors, can for a moment hold such a view.

II. Equally untenable with this is the view that David wrote none of the Psalms.

---

[1] That is, the title of the Book of Psalms: "David" is to be understood as meaning: "David and other writers." (T.)

As an almost necessary corollary to his view of the Maccabean Psalms, Olshausen asserts that there are clearly no Psalms in our collection so old as the Davidic-Solomonic era; while Cæsar Lengerke, in his Psalm Commentary, a book of no value save as a literary curiosum and unworthy of a scholar who could write as ably as he did of Jewish antiquities, maintains that it is a mistake to suppose that David was a religious poet at all.

Probably there is no one here to whom it would be necessary to prove the Davidic authorship of a large number of the Psalms. Fortunately we are able to do so on purely literary ground, which of course is alone recognized by those who deny all Davidic authorship.

Kuenen and the Dutch scholars who are endeavoring to restore the history of Israel, tell us that the appearance of Amos was the dawn of the religious consciousness of the nation, and his prophecy the earliest literature which has come down to us. But here, as elsewhere, the famous eighth century theory is proving too much for those who have elaborated it with such pains, and it is only fair to add, with such skill. Granted the sure authenticity and trustworthiness of the eighth century prophets, we have all the ground which any scholar needs for proving that there must have been a precedent literary period. Quite to the point here we find David mentioned in Amos vi. 5, an authority which Kuenen, by the very terms of his theory, can not deny, as having been a famous musician. We can, moreover, prove that he was no mean poet, even leaving the Psalms out of consideration, and without regard to the Chronicles, which the newer school refuse to consider an authority. There is not to be found in the Greek elegiacs, a song with sentiment so exquisite, or feeling so tender, as his elegy on Saul and Jonathan, a poem whose choicest beauty has evaporated in our English translation. In the lament over Abner we have a beautiful fragment from a longer song, and in II. Samuel xxiii., we have preserved still another poem of David's, which has not been included in the Psalm collection. The conception of him by the Hebrew historians is as the chief master of their lyric song; not creator of it, for it had existed long before him—but as the one whose poetry opens the golden age of their literature with a perfection of form which made it the model for all the later time. If there be anything in the past attested by the evidence of history or the unanimity of tradition, it is that David was a poet.

And when I say this I am not unaware that the newest histories of Israel characterize David as an oriental despot unredeemed by any virtue or any spark of genius; that it is charged by scholars of great learning that he was a freebooter who displaced his rightful sovereign, and that the annalists employed by and attached to his dynasty have written his history at the expense of Saul, who was really the one great man of the early time. I further know that the rising school of Shemitic mythology whose centre is at the Hungarian University of Buda-Pesth, and which has not a few followers in England, regard him as a mythical character, whose main features are borrowed from the Sun-myth; for example, that his fight with Goliath, like the fable of our Scandinavian ancestors, where Thor throws his hammer into Hrungnir's forehead, is but a symbol of the ray of the dawning shooting through and dispersing the heavy overhanging mist of the night, and so on to the end of the chapter. But this is not serious history. There is scarcely any character in the olden time painted with such fidelity of detail, such manifest honesty in concealing none of the darker lines, as is the character of David by the compilers of the books of Samuel. If we know any figure of history we know his. If it is all a myth, as the latest school tells us, there is then no history of the world save as it commends itself to our own subjective judgments; history is but the internal panorama of our mind and no longer an external series of acts and phenomena. I cannot go further now in speaking of David's personality; the few scholars who deny the possibility of

Davidic Psalms do so on ground we are forced to regard as untenable. The great majority of scholars accept, as clearly proven, the Davidic authorship of some Psalms, but differ very widely as to the number.

We have in our present Psalm Book seventy-three Psalms, which, according to their inscription, have been taken from the older Davidic Collection: the entire First Book, thirty-seven in accurate count; eighteen in the Second Book; only one in the Third Book, and two in the Fourth Book, then rising again to fifteen in the Fifth Book.

Of the thirty-four inscriptionless and anonymous Psalms, there is no ground to believe that any came from this "Davidic Collection," and there is no one of them in regard to which we do not have convincing reasons for saying it cannot have come from the Davidic age. Jerome makes a mistake, when, in his letter to his brother ascetic Cyprian, he establishes as the canon of authorship, "that all Psalms without inscriptions must be referred to the last author named."

It is neither suitable to this time nor place to discuss the various views of inspiration; suffice to say it has not freed men from the invariable personal equations of their character and their style. Isaiah writes the purest Hebrew; the Chronicler blunders in his grammar, and the Ecclesiast has a half Aramaic patois; the author of Job soars to the heights of poetry;

the writer of Ruth has a prose style clear as crystal, while Ezekiel grows involved in his endless figures, and Esther wearies one with its platitudes; Samuel and Kings are set together with some regard to conciseness and historical sequence, while Genesis ever anew surprises the reader with the artlessness of its compiler in his use of his material. Such being the case, the sufficiency of the canons gained from the study of other literatures must be granted, else there can be no study of the Hebrew writings as literature. Of course this would not preclude their study from other, perhaps more valuable, standpoints, but it would raise an insuperable barrier against any such purely literary study as these lectures are alone engaged with.

Taking up the Psalms of the Davidic Book, scholars have been accustomed, first of all, by means of the dozen or so poems which, from internal setting or external allusion, have a consensus in their favor as of Davidic authorship, to fix what they call David's style of writing, and make this the standard for judging the other poems of the collection. Now style, though, on the whole, the surest purely literary test of authorship, is not a complete one, especially when dealing with ancient literature. I doubt, if the writings of the English Poet-Laureate should have the good fortune to survive two thousand years, and then be the sole remains of English letters from the Victorian period, whether any one will be inclined to refer the " In Memoriam " and " The Princess " to the same author. Perhaps they will say they have been placed together through the misapprehension of some later editor, while the " Northern Farmer " will doubtless be rejected as spurious by all, and made the point of many an argument as to the decay of English speech. In the study of any ancient literature, the argument from literary style can only be used with the greatest caution. It has broken down in the literary study of the Hebrew Scriptures just at a point where most was expected of it—in the comparison of the earlier and later chapters of Isaiah.

In studying the Psalms of this Davidic collection, scholars too often have used the argument in a logical circle, by first choosing poems which, from certain peculiarities of style, approved themselves as Davidic, and then making them a norm for determining all the rest. Style has, and ever will have, so long as literature is studied, great value when employed by cautious hands. There is essential to its use a delicate æsthetic perception and a wide knowledge of literature, such as are combined in very few. It furnishes, when one can rightly use it, complete subjective satisfaction as to the age and authorship of a literature, but is not objectively conclusive unless confirmed by the further evidence of grammatical form and historical allusion. The argument from grammatical form is alone of value to the specialist who is conversant with the niceties of the language, but the argument from historical allusion appeals to every one, with quite as much force to the student of a translation as to the student of the original. For example: we have a very celebrated paraphrase of the Pentateuch—the Jerusalem Targum—which has sometimes been referred to a period prior to our era. When scholars came to study it critically, they found allusions to Muhammed, to the rise of Islam, and even to the capture of Constantinople. Surely it will be clear to the dullest mind that the literary form in which we have this work must be subsequent to the events to which it alludes. Or again, take an example from our own English literature: you all well know that there are certain plays which were long attributed to Shakspere, but on examination it has been found that they contain allusions to a later time. Now the moment this was proven on sufficient grounds, the Shaksperean authorship was given up. In other words, in all literary investigations, an unmistakable and clearly proven allusion to some well known event, shows the piece in question to be contemporaneous with or subsequent to such event. When to the argument from historical allusion we add that of grammatical form, and style, we have a chain of evidence which is unbreakable. We are fully justified in applying the same canons in any critical investigation of the Hebrew literature, taking care however to exclude the prophetic writings, which, by their definition, include such an element of introspective and prospective vision as to place them beyond measurement by the standard of "historical allusion." At least, I speak for myself as to the prophetic writings. I know it is not an exception which would be allowed by very many, who see no more in the prophetic intuition than an acute discernment and political sagacity; but this we will discuss at another time. There can be no objection to applying these canons in the study of those works which make no pretence to be prophetical, so least of all to the study of the Psalms.

Let us apply them then to this Davidic Collection we are now investigating.

First, we have the argument from style, and this seems to show, that certain of these poems are probably not of Davidic authorship—of course by itself this establishes no more than a probability. The Davidic style as we learn it from undoubted Davidic Psalms, such as viii., xv., is terse, vigorous and rapid. When we come to a Psalm whose style is heavy, whose metre is halting, and whose rhetoric is turgid, as Psalm lxxxvi.,—we have reason, if there be no external convincing grounds, to assume that it must be from some other author. David's writings attest him as a man of original mind; his poetry is easy and limpid, showing no trace of conscious effort. When we come to Psalms like lxxxvi., civ., cxliv., roughly pieced together from many different sources which we can trace, elaborated with conscious effort and yet with so artless a skill that the joints of the workmanship can even now be discerned, it is but fair to assume, as above, that it must be from some other hand than the master one of David.

Again, David's Psalms show a unity of treatment and consecution of thought; when therefore we come to a Psalm where there is a sudden break in the style and which is made up of two parts radically different in treatment, as Psalm xxiv., it is not unwarranted to say that here are either two Psalms of David which have been later united, or it is the product of some later singer.

Finally, the argument from style helps us on the positive as well as the negative side. Psalm xxiii., the choicest gem of the Hebrew lyric, has had its Davidic authorship disputed for many centuries, yet in the turn of its expression it brings to a student of style a flavor so unmistakably similar to the proven Davidic Psalms, that he has little hesitation, despite the arguments from its peculiar vocabulary, to say that it is David's.

The second canon which we may apply in the investigation of our Davidic Book, is the one from grammatical form. As I said in the second hour, all language, like the human organism whose peculiar faculty it is, has a birth, growth and decay, and the traces of this growth in the inflection and form of words is one of our surest landmarks in ascertaining the age of any piece of literature at issue.

The English language has grown and changed in the four hundred years between Chaucer (1400) and Pope (1744.) The grammatical form in the poetry of Pope and Gray (1771) and Thomson (1748) is so essentially different from that of Chaucer and Lydgate (1461) and Occleve (1454), that no one, for a moment, even were the knowledge of the authorship lost, could refer the Canterbury Tales to the age of the House of Hanover, or the Elegy in a Country Church Yard to the age of Richard II.

There must have been a similar growth in the Hebrew during the still longer five hundred years between David and the Exile, say, 1055–555 B. C. Did we possess the Psalms in their original shape, we should be able, with reasonable surety, to make use of this canon in determining the age, and thus in a measure the authors of the several poems of the "Davidic Collection." I showed you, however, that the old Hebrew literature has been alone preserved to our time in a service book prepared as late as the sixth century after our era, in which all that was characteristic in grammatical form has been flattened out into a uniform liturgical pronunciation. We can therefore make little use of this standard. Though it has been used occasionally by scholars, the results have possessed no assured value. The only instances where it may suggest a clue as to the age of the poems are Psalms ciii., cxxiv., cxxxix.

David lived in an age when the language was still spoken and written in its purity. He himself writes with classical exactness. When we find one or two Psalms of the collection whose grammar shows traces of Aramaic forms, it is not unfair to conclude that they may have come from some author exposed to Aramaic influence, or from a time when the Aramaic had commenced encroaching on the Hebrew.

Would any scholar be blamed for referring a Spanish poem, whose grammar betrays the influence of the Arabic, to a period when it would have been possible for the Arabic to have exerted an influence on the Spanish? Would any literary study of the Spanish be possible, were this disallowed?

The last canon in our investigation of this Davidic collection is that of historical allusion. If a German poem contains allusions to the horrors of the Thirty

Years War, and the burning of Magdeburg by its inhabitants to escape the sack of Tilly, we at once conclude that it must belong either to a contemporaneous or to a subsequent era. Let me ask you how we should treat poems in this Davidic collection, making no pretence to be prophecy, which might happen to contain allusions to the Exile not as future, but as a present and stern reality.

We do find such allusions in the last verses of several of the Psalms, as xiv., li., and this has led many scholars to refer these poems to the time of the Exile. *A priori* there can be no reason why the old collection, "The Sacred Songs of David," could not contain hymns from any period during five hundred years, but in respect to these Psalms there is another and more adequate explanation, which shows us that even the argument from historical allusion may not be conclusive unless accompanied and confirmed by that from style and grammatical form. The style of the earlier verses in each of these Psalms is clearly different from that of the last verse, in which is found the prayer for deliverance from the captivity, and for the return of the people to Zion. The style of the first verses is so strikingly similar to David's, that we conclude that they may have been older poems which were in frequent use during the Exile, when they received as a final refrain or doxology this last verse; that this was so commonly sung with them, that it was taken by the compilers into our collection, and by a mistake of later editors and scribes it came to be treated as part of the poem rather than its liturgical refrain. Of course the question still remains as to the authorship of the previous verses, in which the style has created an impression in favor of the Davidic authorship.

But there is another class of Psalms whose historical allusions are too ingrained in the poem itself to be explained fairly in any such way. Several Psalms, as lxix., lxxi., seem to refer so clearly to the situation of Jeremiah when imprisoned for proclaiming the approach of the storm of foreign invasion, whose lowering clouds his eye alone had been opened to behold, that most scholars, with justice, refer them to the period of Jeremiah. When they further discover that the phraseology and turn of expression are similar to that which is found in Jeremiah's prophetic writings, you perceive, that in the absence of authoritative proof to the contrary, it creates as strong evidence as we can have to the authorship of any piece of literature which has come down to us from antiquity.

We might go through the Davidic Book, as scholars have often done, with these three canons of style, grammatical form, and historical allusion, but we can no longer dwell upon it.

Its result has been a double one:

I. It has shown on literary and historical ground, not alone of value, as too many arguments used in the discussion of this question are, for one party, or one confession, or one time, that a large number of poems in the Davidic Book are, beyond question, of Davidic authorship.

II. It has shown that standards such as we deem authoritative in all other literary investigation compel us to refer some of the poems to a later author, whom in a few cases like that of Jeremiah just mentioned, we are able to fix, but in the majority of cases we have to leave undetermined.

As to the number of David's own compositions, I personally side with the more conservative view which assigns him the much larger number of Psalms in this collection. I will not however conceal from you, that the ablest defender within our century of the historical and poetical character of David, Professor Ewald, in his Commentary on the Psalms, which will ever remain a monument to his own poetical genius, can not see his way clear to assign to David more than a small number.

Scholars differ widely as to the number of David's personal compositions, from the fact that in the

Davidic Book are so many Psalms of uniform and colorless style which can be attributed with equal justice to David, or to any one else; so many poems destitute of all local setting and allusion which may equally belong to the Davidic or some later time.

There is a good story told in a Mediæval Jewish poem—a sort of Inferno one might call it—where David, who has grown anxious to know how he has been entreated by the after time, is represented as sending out for all who have commented on his book to appear before him. He finds, as we might expect, that all the commentators have been consigned to the Inferno—whence being hastily summoned, they come running, books in hand, David Kimhi at the head, make obeisance before him, and open their books. Thereupon David asks them to show him what they have written on the sixty-eighth Psalm,—perhaps the hardest of the collection. No sooner do they hear the sixty-eighth Psalm mentioned, than they fall out among themselves, first with words, then with blows, as to whether David could have written it, and still contending, the king drives them, in disgust, away from him. The story would not lack application even now.

There are many Psalms well-nigh as doubtful or difficult as the sixty-eighth, in regard to which scholars differ irreconcilably, and where their previous training, their habit of thought, and their literary method can alone determine their opinion. A conservative mind will probably refer all the doubtful Psalms to David—one more radically disposed will perhaps refer none of them to him. Therefore it is that among scholars who acknowledge Davidic authorship, there is such disagreement as to the authorship of the Psalms of the "Davidic Book."

It is hard to make an estimate of the differing views—perhaps of the seventy-three Psalms borrowed by our Psalter from the older collections, the most conservative attribute to David himself between fifty and sixty, the more radical no more than eight or ten. It is a question which can only be decided for each through a patient, minute and loving study of the separate poems.

However the historian may settle David's character, whether he be a just ruler, great in his own right, or an astute usurper who has snatched the laurels of another, his authentic writings will hand him down to all future time as the world's greatest master of lyric song. He has entered closest to the heart of nature; he has caught, as none other, its ever manifold expression; he has soared nearest heaven, and lifted mankind toward divinity.

LECTURE V.

In the closing moments of the last hour I was speaking to you of the "Davidic Song Book." I endeavored to make clear to you that it was one, probably the chief one, among the many song books of the præ-exilic Temple, to whose other service books, as the "Songs of the Sons of Korah" and the "Songs of Asaph," I will later refer. I further showed that from this older "Davidic Book" the collectors of our present post-exilic service book, or rather books, for there are five of them, have borrowed almost half their songs—seventy-three out of one hundred and fifty.

Permit me, as supplementary to add one or two remarks: 1st. It is not probable that the Psalter contains all the songs of the older book. It seems to have been a source which was drawn on gradually and in various measure by the several compilers of the five books which make up our later collection.

We saw that the first book was composed entirely from the " Davidic Songs," and was doubtless a selection of its choicest and most familiar melodies, and that in the second book another draft of eighteen songs is made on the same source. For some reason unknown to us the compiler of the third book borrows but a single song from this præ-exilic book ; and in this he is followed by the compiler of the fourth book, who borrows but two—both, in common, seemingly preferring to draw on the stores of religious melody of the people which until this time had not been collected and which naturally, to a great extent, were anonymous. The much later compiler of the fifth book again borrows for his collection, designed largely for choral and liturgical use, fifteen melodies, which were evidently used in much the same way in the older collection. Of course no one can, of knowledge, assert that our Psalter does or does not contain all the melodies of the Davidic collection used in the worship of the præ-exilic Temple. All we can say is that the way in which the compilers of the present book use the hymns seems to imply that they borrowed only such as they considered of value for the re-established Temple worship.

We have shown before that the guiding principle in their collection was a religious one—their only aim being to furnish a suitable service book for the worship of Jehovah. The Psalter cannot be said to be an anthology of the best Hebrew poetry, even of the best religious poetry, for much that we know must have been accessible to the collectors, as the Song by the Sea and the Song of Deborah, as poetry superior to anything in their collection, has not been made use of.

If we can make clear to ourselves the design of their collection, we can then understand why they borrow so largely from the worship books of the First Temple, which had grown sacred and familiar to the people. In the present lies mirrored all the history of the past, be it for politics, or art, or literature. There is no school whose discipline is so essential to the student of letters as is a knowledge of the method of his own age and race. Grote, by his conversance with the English finance and politics of his own time, made clear many problems in the history of the Greek states which had for centuries baffled scholars who had approached it alone from the standpoint of their Greek studies. Perhaps a study of the old Temple hymns from the standpoint of a modern hymn collector might yield equally valuable results, for with all the differences of conception and expression peculiar to an alien race and an early time, the Hebrew hymn collectors of twenty-three centuries ago seem to have followed the same canons in their collection as any skilful and painstaking collector would use at the present. And let me illustrate this by showing you the *method* in which they treated the hymns which they have collected.

You well know the loving care with which a modern collector gathers from all sources those hymns, which through use or association have grown sacred, with what diligence he seeks the earliest form through their manifold versions and improvements by later editions, with what minute accuracy he collates and restores the text, how he searches musty archives to establish date and authorship, and acquaints himself with all the contemporaneous history that he may understand clearly their local allusions. Could we conceive of our Psalm collectors, whoever they may have been, acting in somewhat the same way, I believe they would be more human to us without being one whit less inspired. We have, in the Psalms themselves, convincing evidence that their literary workmanship was not unlike that of collectors in the present day.

The thirteenth poem in the first book, numbered as fourteenth in our English Bibles, is a very celebrated one, more perhaps for its general sentiment than its poetical expression, and in the early time, as its refrain in the last verse shows, it was a very popular and familiar one. The text, judging from the few marks which can guide one, has been edited with care. Quite remarkably we find the same poem (the fifty-third in the English version) in the second book (xlii.–lxxii.) which as we have seen, was made later than the first and by another hand. Whether the compiler of the second book was aware of the existence of the same Psalm in the former collection or not, we have no means of knowing. Of great value however, for our insight into the literary method of the compilers, is the fact that with the undoubted similarity of the two Psalms patent to any one even in the English, we find so many slight differences as to compel us to assume that both collectors could not have had before them the same text of the poem. (And let me remark here for those conversant with the Hebrew text that differences such as this must be referred back to the compilers of the separate books; as with the collection of the five books in one common Psalter or service-book came a tendency toward unification of the textual diversities, which shows itself in several noteworthy ways.) When we minutely scrutinize the fifty-third Psalm, we find its textual diversities from the fourteenth precisely of such a kind that did they occur in a modern hymn collection, we should say that both the collectors have had before them the same old hymn; that the fourteenth has been edited with great care and from good manuscripts, while the fifty-third has been edited from imperfect manuscripts, or, more probably, taken from some later hymn book where it had suffered the attrition necessarily consequent upon constant use. A similar case occurs in the great mediæval hymn, the *Dies Iræ*, which presents two versions almost precisely in a similar relation to one another as are the fourteenth and the fifty-third Psalms. Is there any reason why the same should not be true for our Psalm collection? If it is not true, how then shall we explain the diverse editing of the same poem?

Or again, Psalm xl. is one of the longer Psalms, whose heavily drawn out lines produce a feeling of satiety utterly foreign to the impression of gracefulness and ease which come to us from the acknowledged Davidic Psalms; its authorship has also been long in dispute on the ground of external allusion. But this is not to our point here. What we wish to call your attention to is that Psalm lxx., is no more than the final verses of Psalm xl., which have been borrowed by the collector of our second book for a purpose which no one could ever divine from the senseless translation of the inscription in the English version — "to bring to remembrance." As the original inscription informs us, it is a choral refrain sung by the priest as the incense cast on the altar began to rise with its sweet savor toward heaven. You may know that there is a not dissimilar choral sung now in some of the oriental churches at the kindling of the incense. In this case the collector has not borrowed the entire song in the shape in which, as we know from Psalm xl., it existed in the older book, but has merely selected the few verses from it which seemed to him best adapted for his new choral; the marks of his workmanship being so clear that even a tyro can perceive them. The treatment of the older poem is not unlike that of the well known "Mother dear, Jerusalem," selections from which are often made use of for recessionals or doxologies. The compiler of Psalm lxx., evidently had before him the same text as the compiler of Psalm xl.; the minute differences between the two Psalms show that he allowed himself to change in the fragment those references to the body of the poem which would have rendered it unfit to be used as a separate piece. Does he not thus unconsciously, and therefore most convincingly, disclose his literary method as one precisely similar to that which you or I would now make use of under like circumstances? Once more—

We have said that the fifth and last book of our Psalter (cvii.–cl.) was much later than the other books and was designed as a liturgical supplement to them, perhaps not unlike the supplemental collection of chants which we now so often see at the close of the hymn books of some Protestant bodies which are hovering on the verge of liturgical song.

When we examine the second poem in this collection (Psalm cviii. in the English version) we find it composed of fragments from two poems in the second book, with a single new introductory verse of its own—verses 2-6 being identical with Psalm lvii., 8-12; verses 7-14 identical with Psalm lx., 7-14. The "make-up," as an artist would say, betrays the method of the collector of the fifth book. If you will compare the opening verses of Psalm cviii., with the corresponding verses of Psalm lvii., you will see that he has borrowed them, even to the final liturgical refrain, which could hardly have been added ere Psalm lvii. had been adapted to the Temple worship. If you will then compare in Psalm cviii. itself, verses 2-6 with verses 7-14, you will find even in the English a radical difference between the two fragments in style, in treatment, and in situation. The first is a fragment from a peaceful pastoral idyl—the second, a fragment from a song breathing of war, whose very measure reechoes the din of the camp. They possess no common idea which would suggest their union, while placed together as they are, without any effort toward unity of treatment or any trace of design to form from them a new poem, we are forced to conclude that they were united for some purely liturgical purpose. Had we the phenomena exhibited by the text of Psalm cviii., as compared with Psalms lvii., lx., presented in any modern collection, we should without hesitation say that the collector of the liturgical supplement had before him the older hymn book from which, for some liturgical purpose, he had taken these two fragments. When we found further in one of the fragments a refrain first added to the original hymn by the compiler of the previous hymn book, would it not be conclusive evidence that the liturgical collector has made this later hymn book his source, and not gone back to the original? I leave it with you to decide whether for literary phenomena, for which, when occurring in our own day, we have a clear explanation, we must, when occurring in our Psalm collection, form some new theory.

I have thus endeavored briefly to present some few of the clues which rightly followed will lead us into the secret of the literary methods of the post-exilic Psalm-collectors. I have not striven to present the strongest points, but rather those where the evidence lay on the surface, and might, in some measure, be estimated at its proper value even by those who have only the English version at their control. Did time permit and were I speaking to an audience who could follow the detail of linguistic minutiæ, on which every literary investigation of value must be founded, I imagine a convincing case could be made out.

In these lectures I have repeatedly had occasion to say that we are dealing with Hebrew literature solely as literature and can not discuss the varying views of inspiration. Am I asked what effect this proved editorial and literary growth of our Psalter has on its inspiration, I reply none at all, but further, and most important of all, that it must first be settled in whom inspiration inheres and just to how many it extends. I presume there are few, if any, of us who would be disposed to deny inspiration to the original form in which these poems came from their authors, but whatever our views may be on this point, none of you can fail to see what difficulties arise the moment we extend this principle to the editors. It has been the rock on which the varying confessions have gone asunder. The moment inspiration has been predicated of the first remove from the original authors, it has seemed impossible to draw an authoritative line. The Latin church by the authority of the Tridentine Council predicates inspiration of Jerome's translation; the oriental churches regard the Greek Septuagint as of final resort, while, till the present day many people of our English tongue hold as authoritative a version, which though in the main correct, in many obscurer passages gives not only not the words but not the sense of the original. I imagine that those of you to whom inspiration means most will agree with me that it must reside in the original, and will also agree with me in the effort to press back, through the literary form in which later editors have cast the writings, to the *ipsissima verba* of the authors. It is generally granted that the form in which all the early Hebrew literature has come to us is that into which it has been cast by later editors, while the manifold differences of readings in each and all the books attest the changes of text which have come in by the hand of copyists.

The literary study of the Hebrew, or the investigation of the method through which its writings have assumed their present shape, at no point therefore trenches on any rational theories of inspiration which may be sacred to any one. So let us now press back one point further and ask what this Davidic Book is on which the editors of our Psalter have drawn so liberally for their collection.

I have said that it was one of the books of the earlier Temple service. This is shown by many musical expressions in the inscriptions and the liturgical refrains of the Psalms themselves which were borrowed by our Psalter collectors as an integral part of the songs which they took from the older book.

It was therefore not a collection of Davidic poems but a service-book which had been used in the Solomonic Temple worship.

It was called "Sacred Songs of David," not because it was composed exclusively of Davidic songs, but because David either inaugurated the collection, or his songs were its largest element. It contains no poem older than the time of David, so in any account we may make of it to ourselves we need not antedate his reign; of the previous development of poetry among the Hebrew people I will speak when I come to take up the *form* of the poems. The collector of the third book does, it is true, begin his collection with a poem of Moses whose authenticity has been doubted by very many scholars, but for whose later origin there is no conclusive literary ground save we accept the *stat nominis umbra* theory of Moses common in the Leyden school. This poem of Moses, however, does not come from the Davidic collection, but has been taken from some source which is not known to us, perchance the old song book—the סֵפֶר הַיָּשָׁר *Sepher hayyashar*—the "Book of Valor," (حَمَاسَة *Hamasat*—"heroic poetry,") which is quoted from so often in the early historical books.

The fables of the Talmud that some of the inscriptionless Psalms are by Adam and Noah, are too worthless to be more than mentioned; disproven without further words by the fact that neither of these could have spoken or written Hebrew, which had not evolved itself as a dialect of the mother Shemitic tongue until long after their time. We come then to the period of David as the time when the Davidic Book must have had its origin.

The eulogies which are lavished upon David as the creator of religious song are founded on misapprehension or incorrect information. In the last hour we studied briefly his poetical character, and saw that as the great master of lyric song he needs no laurels plucked from his predecessors; it would be as little to say for him that he created religious song as it would be to say for Shakspere that he created the English drama. It is granted but to few rare spirits, as Dante, to create a literature and remain its master and model for all future time. We cannot anticipate what we have at some future time to say of the rise of religious song, but four centuries before David was born, the priest Pentaur had sung the immortal hymn to Amun-Ra, the source of life and light, in which we, three thousand years later and of a different creed, could well greet, morning by morning, the rising sun. Even in the Shemitic orient and among the Hebrews themselves there had been not a few religious singers ere the master appeared, some of whom, as Deborah, touched a few keys with more power than he himself ever attained.

David's appearance on the stage of history was not unlike to that of our English master Shakspere. Both came just at the same linguistic period; Shakspere, when the purest English born of Saxon and Norman was still undefiled—David when Jewish, born of the patois of the south had not yet been touched by the blight of Aramaic; Shakspere at the opening of the heroic age of England, when Englishmen, weary of being rent asunder by intestine feuds, begin to feel for the first that they are a nation and are just entering on a splendid career of colonization which is to carry their power and language round the world—David, when Israel, weary of the unrest and anarchy of the Judges, feels for the first its nationality and begins its brief period as a foreign power; Shakspere, at the close of a religious reformation which had upturned and reshaped English society—David at the close of the religious reformation under Samuel, which, if rightly understood, would seem more remarkable to us than the Protestant Reformation of Europe. Both came at epochs known in literature as creative, at periods when both their peoples were entering on a new era, when the national life coursed quickest, and the spirits of the people were most buoyant.

But even with all the likeness in the surrounding of the two masters, it is in their mind and art we must look for the closest link between them, and when I say this I am aware of the necessary unlikeness of mind between a dramatic and a lyric poet—perhaps the two masters are the nearer together because each so strikingly illustrates this dissimilarity. The dramatist who deals with human passion must know men and human motives, that he may be able to reproduce, in pantomime, the mimic play of life. Never was there one who knew and drew life as surely as did our English master—there is hardly a poet who lacks this element as much as David. The lyrist is nothing if not a subjective artist —the world to him is a panorama, pictured by the imagination, before the illumined eye of his mind. He is the creature of the moment, his art is to catch on his canvas the rainbow colors of his distant horizons ere they fleet from view. Necessarily in painting nature he reproduces himself, and we have elegy or idyl as the poet himself is grave or gay. Scarcely in any literature do we have so subjective an artist as David; one whose poetry is more the expression of the passion of the moment, or one who so constantly betrays his personal emotion; perhaps in no literature do we have so objective an artist as Shakspere, or one whose personality so completely withdraws itself behind the characters he causes to pass before us.

And yet with this dissimilarity there is a similarity

in their art, for each was perfect in its kind – in their mind, for each was most delicately adapted for its work. Had David possessed the dramatic mind, the world would have lost the eighth Psalm—had Shakspere possessed the lyric mind, the world would have lost Hamlet, and I know not which were the greater loss. They may stand forever together as the two great masters of the world's poetry, dissimilar, no doubt, in that they fill different spheres, but still alike in that in their art they are equally great.

In the last hour I said that David was an original artist, and so he was. He created for the Hebrew lyric a new and perfect form which his successors could only strive to imitate and approach. But as every other literary artist, he drew on the stores of the past. We can trace very clear recollections of the older "Song by the Sea" in several of his poems, and did we have more remains of the secular and religious poetry current in his day, we should doubtless find this only the more confirmed. Whether he collected his own poems or not, we do not know; busied as he was in the organization of the service for the Temple he was not suffered to build, possibly he may have collected, doubtless he did collect, a book for the liturgical worship. Judging from David's literary method shown in the composition of his Psalms, we should have reason to believe that he drew on the stores of older religious hymns in the composition of his book. It may have contained the old songs so freely made use of by the compilers of the historical books; he may have drawn on the still earlier collections, the "Book of Valor" and the "Book of War Songs," which the annalists of his time so frequently quote from. We are told that there were religious מִשָׁלִים, *Moshelim*, troubadours who wandered from village to village among the people, singing the melodies of the desert and the olden time. It is not impossible that his book contained some of these religious songs which had been handed down by word of mouth.

David's reign, with all the brilliancy of its foreign conquests, was internally a failure, and ended disastrously. Napoleon once said of a monarch known to you all that one *trouvère* on the throne would suffice Europe for a century. Israel showed by its constant sedition and revolts, that it had grown weary of its poet king who could rule neither his family nor his subjects. It was alone his prætorian guard of foreign mercenaries, the Crethi and Plethi, and the cunning of his councillors, which saved him from the revolt of Absalom. First in the after time, when his foreign conquests had all been lost, and Israel, divided against itself, had fallen a prey to the stranger, men began to look back with pride and sorrowful longing to the son of Jesse, who from a shepherd boy had risen to be a king who had conquered their enemies and made Israel great.

Whether Solomon cast the Davidic Book into a new shape for the more elaborate ritual of the Temple, built for him by Tyrian artificers, we do not know. Some have gone so far as to state the theory on the ground of the seventy-second Psalm, that he issued a new edition of it for the dedication service of the Temple, a good instance of the many theories of the commentators, reminding one of the attempt in palæontology to restore a mammoth from a single tooth.

Solomon, if we consider authentic the writings ascribed to him, was not a lyric poet. His habit of mind tended rather to that sententious and aphoristic gnomic poetry, which in the Orient, where it has been the most common species of literature from the earliest times to the present, is always connected with his name as its great master. It seems probable that the two Psalms lxxii., cxxvii., which in the original bear the inscription "to Solomon," are dedicated to him and not by him, a sense which is well conveyed to the English reader by the "for Solomon" of our versions. The seventy-second Psalm is an invocation of blessing upon him by some contemporary poet whose name is not given us by our Psalter collectors—it is not even ascribed by them to the Davidic Book, though the supplemental note at the end of the Psalm points to their having taken it from there. The Psalm is so clearly dedicated to the king that those who, against language and tradition, insist on regarding the Psalm as of Solomonic authorship, are compelled to assume that he must have written it for his people to sing in his own honor. The one hundred and twenty-seventh Psalm is one of the late Pilgrim Songs whose inscription "to Solomon" or "for Solomon" fails in the Septuagint and many of the early versions; there is reason to believe it is of late origin in the Hebrew. We simply then do not know whether David originally collected his book while Solomon revised and re-edited it or not. As, however, it contained so many later hymns, we must look to some subsequent literary period for its revision into the shape in which it lay before the compilers of our Psalter. There is little difficulty in the quest, for there is but one distinctly literary period subsequent to the time of Solomon.

The reign of Solomon is known in history as the golden age of Hebrew letters and of the Hebrew nation, but one may hear in it the mutterings of the coming storm as clearly as in the reign of Louis XIV. It was indeed a reign of magnificence, and unprecedented wealth flowed into the royal coffers from the shrewd commercial policy of opening up through his territory a new and shorter line to the Phœnician trade. His splendid court, his retinue of wives, the ivory palaces of Jerusalem, bear witness to the wealth and extravagance of the age. But it was, even for the orient, an intensely personal government which the men of Israel with their inbred spirit of liberty could not willingly brook. The people were ground to the earth by the oppressive taxation necessary to maintain the royal state. The tribes of the north, dissatisfied by the aggrandizement of Judah at their expense, even before his death show open resistance to his authority, and are on the verge of a general revolt. In the closing years of his reign he is forced to accept humiliating treaties rather than risk the internal disorder which a foreign war would have brought on. His vain, weak and obstinate successor but garners the whirlwind which his father had sown.

After the northern kingdom had cast off the authority of the Davidic house it seemed as if no other could hold its ground. Dynasty after dynasty of usurpers whose right to the throne was secured by murder, followed and displaced one another in rapid succession—within the first century there are no less than five. It is a history of two centuries of internal disorder which only at intervals ceased that all might unite against the common foe on the north. There was no learned class in the Ephraimitic state, nor if there had been one would there have been the leisure and repose essential to a literary period.

The kingdom of Judah, on the other hand, governed, save for occasional and short intervals, as when a pretender like Athaliah (עֲתַלְיָה) seizes the throne, by the dynasty of David to which the people had grown attached, remained almost exempt from internal disorder. It rarely measured arms with Ephraim without its northern rival's proving too strong for it, and it seems probable that after the fight at Beth-Shemesh,[1] Israel for a number of years held complete control of Judah. The quiet assured by the regular and undisputed succession of its monarchs gave to the smaller state the leisure for internal development, which Israel with its greater power never secured—the Temple and schools of Jerusalem furnished a centre for the literary class which Israel did not possess. Notwithstanding this quiet, there seem to be but two periods of the Jewish monarchy—that of Jehoshaphat and that of Hezekiah—which can lay claim to be regarded in any sense of the word as literary epochs. Jehoshaphat's reign is an afterglow of the glories of the Solomonic age. It was a period

[1] Victory of Jehoash of Israel over Amaziah of Judah. 2 Kings xiv. 11-14. (T.)

of peace and prosperity, but more than all it was a period of educational reform. Its abiding interest to us is the pedagogic commission, which the king sends through the land to reform the public instruction and arrange for the proper primary education of the rural districts, antedating by two thousand years our modern educational reformers. It might of course in a certain sense be called a literary period, but as the movement does not seem to have extended beyond educational reform, I prefer to compare it with the period of the Carlovingian " Missi"[1], and not class it as a distinctly literary time. We have beyond doubt in the Davidic book and thence in our Psalter several songs which unmistakably breathe of this time, but there is no record of any collection of the older literature such as would lead us to refer a revision of the Davidic Temple Book to this period.

The only period between Solomon and the Exile which can be given, with justice, the name literary, is the reign of Hezekiah. Hezekiah is often sketched to us as the Hebrew Pisistratus, one who played in the collection and preservation of Hebrew letters somewhat the same rôle that the tyrant of Athens, who lived a century after him, (Hezekiah 716–687, Pisistratus 600–527), did in collecting the songs of

---

[1] The *Missi* were special judges sent out to inquire into and correct abuses. (T.)

Homer. In studying the character of Hezekiah one gains the impression that he was a man cast in much the same mould as James I. of England —a vain and conscious pedant, whose faith serves him as a matter of controversy rather than a guide of life—in his internal management weak and shifty, by turns despotic and tolerant—in his foreign policy seeking to gain by a tortuous overreaching of his neighbors what directness alone could accomplish, and more than once bringing himself and his state to the verge of ruin. It is here, as so often elsewhere in history, that we have to thank the pedantry and the desire of weak men to be considered as patrons of letters, for the collection and preservation of some of our most priceless remains of antiquity. He appointed a board of scholars to whom he gave commission to collect all the accessible remains of the earlier literature, and to edit them in new and revised form. Have you never noticed even in your English Bibles the note this old commission has left in Proverbs xxv. i? All the last seven chapters of Proverbs have been saved to us by their efforts—were probably collected by them from the old manuscripts which they were collating to establish the text of the book, and added by them as a supplement to the imperfect copies of their own day. The Talmud refers to them the collection and revised edition of all the Hebrew literature existing in their time, but whether this be so or not, we find, as of utmost importance for our present study, that Hezekiah set on foot a reorganization of the Temple worship, and for this purpose had a new collection made of the older Davidic songs. The liturgical inscription of Hezekiah's own poem preserved to us incidentally (Isaiah xxxviii. 9, מִכְתָּב *miktab* for מִכְתָּם *miktam*) renders it probable that this too, was included in the same collection.

We have thus reached the time when the "Davidic Book" was collected substantially into the form in which it lay before the compilers of the post-exilic Psalter. The one or two Jeremianic poems which the book seems later to have contained, came gradually into use in the communities of the Exile, to whose feeling of despairing supplication they gave expression as none of the older songs were able to do.

I trust the sequence of my thought has been clear: that our Psalter as it exists in the Hebrew original and thence in our English translation was the hymn book collected for the worship of the Second Temple; that on *a priori* grounds it was natural to suppose that the collectors of this new praise book would draw largely on the similar books in use in the former Temple. Further, this supposition was shown to be a fact, by the preservation, either in the inscriptions or foot notes, of the names of many of the sources from which they have drawn. Chief among these sources was a book whose very name, "Sacred Songs of David," is preserved to us in the subscription of one of the Psalms.

Taking up then the examination of this Davidic Book, we saw that many of the songs borrowed from it, contain such musical and liturgical notes, as to point to its having been used as a service book in the older Temple worship. We then stated some literary and critical canons whose proper application to the study of this collection can not with justice be disputed. These seemed to show us that the collectors of our post-exilic Psalter drew on the Davidic collection much in the same way that hymn collectors of the present day would draw on any older collection which was accessible to them, and that they made use alone of such hymns or such parts of hymns as were suitable for the later worship. Consequently it is not probable that our Psalter contains more than a selection from the Davidic Book.

We saw that the older book received the title Davidic, from the usage, so common in the Orient, of naming a collection from the one who inaugurates it, or whose contributions form its oldest or most considerable part; that though the Davidic authorship of each and all of these hymns has been sharply disputed, it may be shown on grounds as reasonably assuring as we can have for any ancient literature, that David wrote many, perhaps most of the poems that have been preserved to us from the service-book which bore his name. On the other hand, we saw that a number of the poems in the Davidic Book so clearly belong to a time subsequent to David, that it cannot have lain before our Psalter-collectors in the form into which it was cast by him; that they probably used it in the revised and enlarged shape given it at the reorganization of the Temple-service in the reign of Hezekiah, and to this last view we showed there could be no objection, as we possess at least the Proverbs in the shape in which they were edited by a literary commission which was appointed by the same king.[1]

I believe that this view which I have endeavored to present without laying stress on any point which was not evident or stretching any to an interpretation it would not bear, will clear up for many of you the difficulties which can not but have presented themselves in reading the Davidic Psalms contained in our Psalter. It satisfies completely the demands from the literary side and also all claims which can be made by any consistent theory of inspiration. But even should this particular explanation not be convincing

---

[1] That is, a part of our present book of Proverbs, Prov. xxv.–xxix. (T.)

or adequate, and its flaws no one sees more clearly than myself, any explanation to be satisfactory must lie somewhere in this line. Bear in mind, ere you reject it, that the prevalent extreme conservative view of the Davidic Psalms is only possible by a disregard of their literary form—the radical view is only possible by a denial of their inspiration. I believe that none of us would be willing to take either horn of this dilemma.

There remains now that we have finished (satisfactorily or unsatisfactorily) the discussion of the literary form in which the Davidic Psalms are preserved to us, still another point for consideration, that though without exception they appear in liturgical form and in a service book, there are few of them which were originally composed with this object in view.

Take any modern hymn collection and you will see that none of its grandest hymns were written primarily for a liturgical purpose. They are poems expressing some feeling or sentiment which renders them suitable to be used in worship; when they come to be adapted to a liturgical service, it is frequently with the loss of much of the beauty of the original poem. There are no doubt hymns written for use in the service, but one needs not a poet's vision to discern them. They betray in their measured form, their meagre thought, and their servile following of certain standards of religious expression common to their time, both their origin and design.

The highest lyric song is the spontaneous outpouring of the sentiment, the passion, the intuition of the moment, and has, can have, no end in view outside the utterance of itself. Do you imagine that the mediæval singers could have written their hymns which have become immortal, for the liturgical service of their church? Does not, for example, Xavier's "O Deus ego amo te" bear on its face that it was a rapt vision and contemplation of some solitary singer which was first at a later day taken by the church into its service because it seemed so fit an expression of the feeling of hearts other than the poet's? Or even in our own time was not the tenderest of our modern religious lyrics, "Lead, kindly light," the overflow of expression of the troubled soul of the most gifted Englishman of the last generation? Do any of you imagine that he could of set purpose and in cold blood have composed it or anything like it for a liturgical choral?

In our study of the Psalms we must bear the same in mind. Could David have written the nineteenth Psalm, "The heavens declare the glory of God and the firmament showeth his handiwork," or the unknown author of the one hundred and fourth Psalm have framed his wonderful poetical cosmos for the use of the Temple choir? If you compare them with the

Psalms written for purely liturgical use, of which we have abundance in our Psalter, you can not hesitate with an answer.

It is then as lyric poetry, the immediate, spontaneous, unfettered expression of the feelings which moved the minds of David and other singers, that most of the songs in the Davidic Book had their origin. He who compiled this Temple song book—be it David or Solomon or Hezekiah—selected and adapted from these poems such as seemed suitable for the liturgical service of the Temple.

We have however now pressed our literary inquiry almost as far back as the data in our possession will safely carry us. For the most part we have these poems preserved to us alone in the liturgical form in which they were adapted for the Temple service, and can follow them no further. The comparison of Psalm xviii., with the similar poem in 2 Sam. xxii., which might occur to some of you as furnishing a clue for this investigation is for several reasons of little value. The most important of them is that the compilers of Samuel who lived in the later Jewish kingdom, or more probably at the beginning of the restored State, do not preserve for us the original poem of David, but have borrowed from the Davidic Book precisely the same Temple song of which the compilers of our Psalter have made use. The few variances between the form of the song in Samuel and that in the Psalms may be accounted for by the state in which, through the carelessness of copyists or the abuse and neglect of the rolls, the text of the Books of Samuel has come down to us. It is no longer possible unless we are willing to make use of the somewhat two edged "restorative criticism" so popular with certain French scholars, to ascertain to what extent the Davidic poems have been abridged or amended to fit them to become Temple songs.

That all the Davidic poetry has been preserved in the Davidic Psalms would be improbable from the exclusively religious character and liturgical design of the Temple book, and is conclusively disproven by the fragments of David's poetry we find scattered through the historical books. No doubt he soared to his loftiest height and touched his sweetest key in the religious song, but it is a loss to the world's imagination that the secular poetry of so great a master has perished. Would that we had the songs that the youthful minstrel sang to the troubled king of the old heroes of the people and the wild days of the judges which were just past; his idyls of shepherd life, some of which, preserved in his Psalms, are painted with more skilful touch than ever Theocritus or Bion possessed; his songs of love and the dance, to both of which his nature inclined him; his war ballads from the days that he and his little company of moss-troopers lived in outlawry along the Judean border. David as a poet is an attractive study, but we have given to him, his Psalms, and his Psalm-Book, all the space that we can in justice spare in so brief a course of lectures.

Our Psalter collectors drew on early sources for their service book, other than the "Sacred Songs of David," and to consider these we must pass in the next hour.

LECTURE VI.

In the last hour we endeavored to present to you the ascertainable facts as to the origin and time of compilation of the "Davidic Temple Book" which the Psalter compilers have so largely drawn on. We now must pass on to consider some new problems of interest in connection with our Psalter.

In one of our early lectures we saw that the present Psalter is made up of five distinct books, which at that time I strove to clearly mark out for you. These were not collected simultaneously or by the same hand, but at intervals, one after another, during several centuries and by collectors whose literary methods very widely vary. We have since seen that the first book was taken entirely from older material, being made up of selections from the "Sacred Songs of David"—a hymn book used in the service of the former Temple, in regard to which we have already spoken at sufficient length. It now remains but briefly to consider when and by whom this first book was collected—we will then pass on to the second book.

One of the most celebrated books[1] of the Orient, if not of the world, begins thus: "Moses received the law from Sinai and delivered it to Joshua, (and) Joshua to the Elders, (and) the Elders to the Prophets, and the Prophets to the men of the Great Synagogue." Jewish myth has much to tell us of this great Synagogue of one hundred and twenty members which sat as the supreme arbiter of morals and religion, from the return from the Exile until about the time of Simeon the Just.[2] To them the Jews refer the collection and editing of their sacred writings, and in this they have been followed by the unanimity of tradition in the Christian Church, which here as most often elsewhere, when the Old Testament is concerned, is an unacknowledged loan from the Jews. When we examine the earlier Jewish writings we find the accounts given of this body contradictory, confused, and projected

---

[1] The tract of the Mishna called *Pirke Aboth*, "sections of the fathers," that is, "sayings of the fathers," a collection of apothegms uttered by the great rabbis, beginning with Simeon or Simon the Just, about B. C. 300. (T.)

[2] He is by some identified with Simon I., B. C. 310-291, by others with Simon II., B. C. 221-202. The former seems the more probable date. (T.)

into mythical outline. All we can gather is that there was a tradition of some such body who, in the disordered times succeeding the return from the Exile, exercised great influence in reorganizing the worship and collecting and setting in order the older literature.

Cyrus' motive in allowing the return was a natural and largely political one. He doubtless regarded it as a piece of astute statecraft to secure on the border of Egypt a people whose gratitude for restoration to their land would bind them firmly to the Persian monarchy. The exulants return with their range of political and religious ideas greatly enlarged by their contact with the administrative system and dualistic faith of the Persian.

Here, as so often in its subsequent history, Israel showed, with all its wonderful tenacity in holding fast the monotheistic idea which has been its mission to the world, its subtle capacity of adapting itself to the religions and civilizations with which it was environed. It has been said that away from native land and Temple the exiles would naturally have met from time to time, perhaps every Sabbath day, for reading the law or one of the prophetic oracles, and then singing some of the old Temple melodies. But those who hold this view forget how the very idea of worship in the older Judaism was bound up with an appearance before Jehovah in the Temple, or at some holy shrine, and with the attendant sacrifice to Him there. We find no trace of any domestic or communal worship of the people away from the Temple at any period previous to the Exile. Synagogue-worship grew up during the Exile under the influence of the Persians, or perhaps one might phrase it better by saying that the idea of it was first suggested to the Jews through their contact with the Persians, whose worship was not confined as that of the Jews had been to any definite place, but whose custom was, wherever they might be, to come together at fixed intervals and in stated places to read their sacred books, to repeat the ancient prayers, and to chant their religious songs. The idea germinated in fruitful soil, and the synagogue, foreign to the original genius of Judaism, and only as a late exotic transplanted from Parseeism, in subsequent centuries became the distinctive feature of the religion of Israel, and little by little eliminated from it all necessity of the Temple worship. I am not, however, to speak to you at present of the history of the synagogue. I mention it alone with the purpose of calling your attention to the new principle which was introduced into the Jewish worship.

In the præ-exilic times the worship was ceremonial. There had been collected some few books of song for the liturgical chanting of the Temple choirs, but beyond that there was no official collection of their sacred literature, nor was there need of any, for the reading of these writings did not form a stated or usual part of their service. With the growth, subsequent to the Exile, of the synagogue worship, whose essence was not ceremonial but social, consisting chiefly in reading from their sacred literature, there came the necessity for the sake of order and uniformity that this literature should be collected, edited with an assured text, and arranged in a consecutive and convenient form by some body whose authority in such matters would be recognized. There would also speedily arise another necessity of determining what books were adapted from their religious character, to be read with edification or instruction to the people who gathered in these assemblies, and this could alone be decided by those whose position in the theocracy lent weight and authority to their decisions.

There is therefore no inherent reason for refusing credence to the Jewish tradition that there was a body of scholars, under the presidency of the High Priest in connection with the Temple in Jerusalem, whose duty it was to adjudicate on these questions. We must bear in mind however, that our present ideas of a canonical or authoritative collection of the Hebrew writings could not have been that of these post-exilic collectors. Both our idea and name originated under Greek influence at a period subsequent to our era.

The technical name Canon has been derived from the terminology of the Greek schools and grammarians of Alexandria. Canon is a word allied to our English "cane," meaning a rod, a rule, a measure, and hence a standard. By the Alexandrian grammarians there was fixed a certain standard of correct Greek style. All writings which conformed to this were called by them canonical, that is standard, or as we should now say classical. For example, Æschylus was said to be a canonical writer, and it was also said he wrote a canonical style, precisely in the sense that we should now say he was a classical writer and wrote a classical style. No doubt this standard of style was first fixed for literary uses in the Alexandrian schools much as at the present we establish certain standards of correct and elegant English, and those writers who conform to it we call our standard or classical writers.

The name does not come until late into ecclesiastical nomenclature. After the early church councils had set up, whether justly or unjustly it is no part of these lectures to inquire, a certain standard for those writings which might be used in the service, there came gradually into use the technical term of the Alexandrian rhetoricians — canonical—to designate all writings which conformed to this standard. If I mistake not, the name canon, as an ecclesiastical term, is first found in one of the "Festal Letters" of the Alexandrian bishop Athanasius (373),[1] a man whose patient endurance of persecution and whose personal beauty of character, far more than his doctrine, should have secured him the title of Saint. Consequently when we use the terms canon and canonical in regard to the writings of Scripture, we can only mean—if we attach any meaning at all to the words—by canon, a regulative standard for them, set up by some body which we regard as authoritative—by the Canonical Books, such writings as conform to this standard which has been established. The meaning given in a later day to the term canonical book, as one which furnishes men with a standard or guide of life, is foreign alike to the history and etymology of the word. In all the canonical controversies of both the earlier and later time it has been generally conceded that the history of the word is as I have just sketched it, and the conflict has turned on the precise nature of the canon or standard which the Jewish or Christian Fathers established, and the extent of the authority inhering in it.

[1] Athanasius uses the term " canonized" (39th Festal Epistle), which supposes the word "canon;" but it probably occurs earlier than this. (T.)

Essential as would be the investigation and discussion of the Canon, were we studying the final form which the writings have assumed, you perceive that of necessity it cannot be a factor in the present investigation into the method in which the earlier Jewish collectors brought together, arranged and edited the Hebrew literature during the century succeeding the Exile. Not until many centuries after their time did there grow up any fixed canon or standard as we now understand it. Of course the collectors must have had some standard in their work, but we can alone ascertain what this was by an examination of the literature which they have collected.

A careful study of the literature which passed through their hands, and of the way in which they edited it, makes several things apparent as to the design and method of their collection which I can but summarize in a few words, for an adequate development of it would lead us too far away from the main point which these lectures have in view.

It is clear that the chief motive of the collectors, perhaps primarily the sole motive, was to prepare for the various synagogues, a standard book of sacred literature for use in their service. The nature of the collection was determined by the necessity of the synagogue worship. That the collectors had no design of gathering all the sacred literature of the

Jewish people may be made evident by the constant reference in the books which have been preserved to a sacred literature, well known and current in their day, which they made no effort to bring into their collection. For example we have the titles preserved of "The Inspiration of Ahijah," and "The Vision of Iddo the Prophet," (2 Chron. ix. 29) both men whose divine sending and message are familiar to us from the historical books. For some reason unknown to us the collectors did not deem them suitable for reading in the assemblies of the people, so have not made use of them. I do not know how I can make the nature of their collection clearer to you than by saying it was a Lesson Book, not unlike that prepared for the English Church service by a commission of the Anglican clergy. It did not contain all the sacred literature of the Jews, but only so much of it as they considered of edification to the people.

Had we space to speak to you of the gradual growth of the collection, of the Jews of the Dispersion, who, passing from the ecclesiastical authority of this board, read in their worship many books which it refused to permit to be read in the synagogues under its control; of the bitter discussions in this body itself attendant on the endeavor made by many of its members in the first century before our era to withdraw authority from Ezekiel, and the even hotter debate which preceded the licensing of the reading of Ecclesiastes and the Song of Solomon in the century subsequent to our era, there would be manifest to you the whole point we wish to make, namely, that there was a board of scholars and ecclesiastics connected with the Temple at Jerusalem to whose hands was committed the care for the order and uniformity of the worship after the Exile. Should we paraphrase the original name of this body into our modern parlance, we might with justice call it a "board of public worship." Among their numerous labors was the preparation of a book of selections from the older sacred literature for uniform use in the service of the synagogues. This book they arranged in appropriate weekly lessons or sections which are still preserved to us in the original text. It would further be evident that subsequent to their first collection they added, from time to time, several books which seemed suitable for use in the service, and that not until the meeting of the doctors of the Sanhedrin held at Jabne in the year 118, A. D., was it finally determined that the collection be regarded as definitely closed, and no additions to or subtractions from it should be made for all future time.[1]

---

[1] The date of this Sanhedrin is in dispute, but it was certainly after the destruction of Jerusalem; it is spoken of in the Talmud-tract Yadayim v. 3, where the discussions on Ecclesiastes and the Song of Songs are

The Protestant Bibles, as a rule, contain the Old Testament in the form determined on by the council at Jabne, while the Bibles of the old Greek and Latin Churches are based on the old Greek or Septuagint version, and contain a number of books read in the synagogue at Alexandria, which were not allowed by the Jerusalem board or commission to be used in the synagogues which were under their immediate jurisdiction.

I imagine the bearing of this somewhat lengthy prologue will be evident to you all, for it would have been impossible for us to follow the collection of our Psalter, unless we had first learned somewhat of the methods through which it, with the other books, came into the collection of Hebrew literature which we have preserved to us. At some future time I may be able to present to you this whole subject more fully and consequently more satisfactorily.

The action of this body, so famous in history, probably alone had influence on the final shaping of our Psalter out of the five Temple books from which it was made up. At all events, the collection of its First

---

mentioned. It seems, however, that sometime after this the Old Testament Canon was to some extent in a fluid condition; we find, for example, that in the fourth century the Jews are spoken of as reading Baruch in their public religious gatherings (Apostolical Constitutions, v. 20). (T.)

Book (iii.–xli.) must be assigned to a period prior to any in which we can suppose such a body as the great synagogue to have been in existence—to a period contemporaneous with the first return from the Exile under Joshua and Zerubbabel. One gains the impression in reading of this first return that its object was not so much for general colonization and resettlement as for the more specific purpose of rebuilding Jerusalem and restoring the Temple. In the list of those who returned we find no less than five thousand, or a sixth of the entire number belonging to the Temple staff, either as Priests, Levites, Singers, Porters or Nethinim, in which latter some of the expositors of the Latin church see a monkish order, but which were, as the name suggests, merely the Temple slaves on whom fell the menial and unclean service which no Israelite would willingly undertake.

Though they thus return with all their plans matured for the restoration of the Temple, unseen difficulties immediately arose and their main object remained for many years unattainable. The Samaritans, angered by the refusal of their proffered co-operation in the rebuilding of the Temple, make such effectual representations through their attorneys at the Persian court as to the disloyalty of the Jews, that the prosecution of the work is forbidden by the authorities. It was an evil time for the returned Exiles, held under suspicion by the Persian officials—dissension and discord among themselves, blight and famine in the land. But I will not draw the picture which lies sketched in outline for you in the concise and nervous sentences of Haggai. Suffice to say, that during fifteen years they could not lay their hand to the work. Thanks to the enthusiastic patriotism of the prophets, Haggai and Zechariah, the people and their leaders are at last moved to make one more appeal to the Persian court, which receives a favorable reply. The work of rebuilding begun in earnest is eagerly pushed forward, and within four years a modest Temple is completed and dedicated, B. C. 516, sixty years before the arrival of Ezra and the later colonists.

Now in all probability it was for the restored service of this Temple that the First Book in our Psalter was compiled by some one of the early return. Whether by Joshua, who we glean from Zechariah was a man of varied parts, of course we do not know. As we have seen, the collector, whoever he may have been, gathered about forty of the choicer and more familiar melodies from one of the books of the early Temple— "The Sacred Songs of David." As a careful editor he gives to each song an inscription, showing the source from which he had taken it; moreover to several of the more noteworthy of them he adds a note, stating the occasion on which it was composed or the circumstances which gave rise to it. In some few cases these notices are taken from the historical books which we still have, but more frequently from the current belief of the time as to the origin of the Psalm.

Psalm iii., first of an exquisite pair of morn and even songs placed at the opening of the book, is accompanied by the notice that it was written on David's flight from his son Absalom.

Psalm vii., whose pathetic and broken rhythm accords well with the wild melody to which it was set by the Temple choir, has a note by the editor that it was written by David as he learned of the words spoken against him by a certain man named Cush of the tribe of Benjamin. Who this Cush was we do not know. His name is nowhere else mentioned, and the editor evidently has taken his notice from some writing which has not come down to us. He probably was David's enemy at the court who succeeded in poisoning Saul's mind with stories of his disaffection. A number of the modern translators have made sad work of this inscription through a misunderstanding of Cush as a common instead of a proper noun. Luther actually has "a Benjamite colored man," anticipating by several centuries the black Jews of Abyssinia, and not a few translate "the black Benjamite" with a metaphrastic reference to the black-hearted Saul.

Psalm xviii. is the longest of the purely lyric songs in the collection. It is shown to be beyond question Davidic by its appearance in the account of David's life in the historical books. The theophany in the opening lines and an occasional turn of the verse betray the master's hand, but the style is on the whole so broad and repetitious that it betrays as well a hand touched with the palsy of age. The editor tells us in his note that it was written by David at the close of his life when he had been delivered and given rest from all his enemies.,

Psalm xxx. was fixed by the Jewish ritual to be read on the feast of *Hanuka*, or Dedication, that is, the re-dedication of the Temple after it had been defiled by the Syrian troops of Antiochus. The form of inscription in the English version, "at the dedication of the house of David," conveys the wrong impression that this was the occasion of the composition of the song. It belongs however to the purely liturgical notes, found in such abundance in the Psalter as to have led many scholars to imagine that our manuscripts of this book are based on the musically annotated copy of some one of the Temple choir, and states no more than that this Psalm was to be sung on the Feast of Dedication.

We should think much less of David's poetical genius could we believe he wrote Psalm xxxiv., an alphabetic poem bearing the strongest marks of the lamp and artificiality of treatment, the metre by constant straining and the use of obsolete words being forced to so come out that each succeeding verse may begin with a new letter of the alphabet. But to crown all, there seems to be an acrostic in the last line, through which the author discloses himself as a certain Pedaiah (פדיה). In all events there is a prima facie case against the correctness of the editorial inscription, that it was written by David when to escape from Achish, king of Gath, he was obliged to feign insanity, an affliction which in the Orient from the earliest time until the present has been regarded as a direct visitation from God, and secured not only immunity but even consideration for the afflicted one. It is a beautiful principle, which lies at the basis of the regulations for the treatment of the insane in modern Arab jurisprudence, that the mind of one who is insane is in heaven, and so engaged in immediate converse with the Deity that it can give no attention to the body which is on earth. Most scholars, even many whose convictions would lead them to do so unwillingly, have been forced to admit that in the case of Psalm xxxiv., the editor is clearly wrong in his note as to the occasion on which it was composed.

The only remaining editorial inscription in this book is that to Psalm xxxviii., of which I spoke in the last hour. The form of it in our English version "to bring to remembrance" is senseless. The song, as the inscription really informs us, is a choral refrain sung by the officiating priests at the kindling of the incense.

The other inscriptions of this book are without exception musical, and come from the chief musician or some of his assistants in the Temple choir. They will all be considered in their proper place.

There is but one more question of literary interest as to this First Book, and that is as to the arrangement of the songs in it. The Shemitic mind, which so dwells on minutiæ, very naturally sets great store by the formal arrangement of its literary material. Take up any of the poets of the famed cycle of the Moallakât, which stands for Arab literature much as the Nibelungen or the Round Table of good King Arthur does for us—or any of the later poets, as Mutanabbi, the Arab Spenser, or Hariri, the Arab Cervantes, and you will find that their poems have been, without regard to their subject or history, cast by the editors into what are called Divâns—that is certain rubrics where all poems of similar metre or assonance are collected under the same head. To gain this purely formal, almost tabular arrangement, the editors have not hesitated to unite or sever many poems in utter defiance of those literary relations which would form the main evidence, for any Aryan editor. Further study shows this to be a common Shemitic method of editing, and not a few scholars have imagined they could trace a similar metrical arrangement in the several books of the Psalm collection. Though there are some few resemblances of metre between adjacent Psalms, such as might be, were there necessity, construed as an argument for this view, they are so sporadic as probably to be only accidental, and do not furnish sufficient ground for predicating any general principle of arrangement of any one of the five collections in our Psalter. What principle of arranging his material the collector of the first book, or of any of the books had, we no longer know—possibly they had none at all. It does not seem to be the metrical one, elsewhere so common among the Shemitic people; nor is there any discoverable arrangement by author or subject or age, such as we are more familiar with. The elaborate arrangements in many modern commentaries are no more than a reflex of the subjective impression of the commentator.

The Second Book of our Psalter is somewhat smaller than the first, and contains the thirty songs which in our version are numbered from xlii.–lxxii., inclusive. The method of the collector is more eclectic than that of the one who collected the first book, and he draws on sources other than the Davidic Songs.

The most characteristic songs in his collection are the seven he has taken from the "Song Book of the Sons of Korah," from which same source the collector of the third book has borrowed three. These songs from the Korahite book are the most exquisite poetry preserved to us, not only in the Psalter, but any where in Hebrew literature. They exhibit a daintiness of workmanship and delicate sensibility of the niceties of metre which place them side by side with the lyrics of Pindar or Horace. If the highest art reside in form rather than idea, as the latter day critics are now teaching the world, there are probably few literatures which offer such models of pure art as we find in one or two of these poems. The reserve of the poet in conscious power over his material, the delicate touch, the keen sense of the beauty of mere form, the plastic skill which reproduces in word the many-voiced utterances of nature, the evident love of the beautiful for its mere beauty, remind us of the very best of Greek art. It is so un-Hebraic, so un-Shemitic, that one is constantly surprised in reading these poems with the artist's *technique*. Were there a score of poems like the forty-second Psalm, the history of Shemitic art would have to be re-written, and the student of style would have to learn of the Hebrew, rather than the Hellen.

These songs represent a poetry of culture which

finds its end in a perfect and artistic expression of itself. They lack the originality, the breadth, the naturalness of David's poetry. There is no such intuition of nature, no struggling of the thought seeking utterance in words, no painting in grand relief such as we ever find in the work of the master. The art is delicate, elaborated, subtle—in a word it is art, not nature. I have no adequate parallel in mind from our modern verse—perhaps if a comparison at a remove were not unfair, I would say somewhat as the dainty and cameo-like Canzone of Petrarch, as compared with the Divina Commedia, or in our own time and speech, as Swinburne's elaborate and elegant form might be compared with the breadth and originality of the Poet Laureate.

But we must see who these Sons of Korah were. Korah, the son of Izhar, of the tribe of Levi, is known to you through the revolt inaugurated by him against the authority of Moses and Aaron. His own motive seems to have been personal ambition or jealousy at seeing another house of his tribe preferred before his own. His movement, however, did not gain weight or become dangerous until it was joined by the influential chiefs of the tribe of Reuben, Dathan and Abiram, who were smarting under the inferior rôle which their tribe, the first-born to whom of right belonged the leadership, were obliged to play.

They take their stand on ground which to any Bedouin Shemitic people, and above all to the Israelites, would have great weight; that the office of priesthood and right of sacrifice could not be delegated to any particular class of the community, but of necessity belonged to the father or head of each house for his own family. They carry a large number, apparently a large majority of the community with them, but rashly submitting their claims to the test of an ordeal by fire, not unlike that in the middle ages, they are defeated and destroyed in the manner you well know. The narrative, which not many verses further on states in plain terms that "the children of Korah were not destroyed," (Numbers xxvi., 11) seems to imply that none perished save those who attempted the ordeal by fire. However this may be, no attainder seems to have attached to Korah's descendants—Samuel the prophet and reformer was of their lineage, and at the time of Saul they were a numerous and influential clan. They came armed to the support of David's feeble fortunes when at Ziklag, and until the end of the monarchy remain the devoted adherents of the Davidic dynasty. David rewards their fidelity by assigning them a prominent position in the Temple service. They are frequently spoken of in the historical books as being custodians of the Temple, but their position, which now alone concerns us, was as forming a part of the Temple choir and orchestra. From the very necessity of their duties they would receive the best musical culture of their time. The musical art being thus their profession, we can the better understand the evident pains taken by them in perfecting the technical detail of their songs.

They seem to have had a book of their own, whose full title we are not so fortunate as to possess, but which was called, doubtless, by some familiar title, as "The Songs, or Lyrics of the Sons of Korah." Whether this was a Temple book like the "Davidic Book," collected from various sources and adapted to the use of the choir by the Korahites, or whether it was a book containing no more than songs by the members of their own singer family, scholars are still not clear, and probably never will be, as there are not sufficient data in our hands to reach a sure conclusion. The ten songs preserved by our Psalter bear traces of so kindred an artistic tradition and poetical method, that it seems more probable that the "Book of the Sons of Korah" was a book containing only songs by members of this family.

As in the "Davidic Book," no mention is made of the authors of the separate poems, the inscription of the editor stating no more than the collection from which the song was taken. We are, in every case, referred back to the song itself for all information as to age and authorship. Let us glance hastily through the few songs taken from this older Korahite collection.

The first of them is Psalm xlii., or rather xlii.–xliii., for Psalm xliii. is clearly the final strophe of Psalm xlii., which has only been separated from it by the blunder of some copyist. The union of the two Psalms is shown to be necessary by the forty-second's remaining incomplete and fragmentary without the addition of the forty-third—it is shown to be a fact by their being found as one Psalm in all the older and better manuscripts.

The singer is in exile or captivity among heathen enemies to whom his religion is a source of mocking. The situation is in the outlying spurs of Anti-Lebanon. He hears the Jordan gush seething from its fountain heads at Baneas and dash roaring down its rocky defile, cataract calling to cataract, on its way toward Merom. He sees the sunny dome of Hermon rising before him, but deems it of less beauty than the little hill of Zion, where rises the city and Temple of his affection. He is one of the Temple singers, who recalls with fondest recollection the time when among his brethren he had led with music and song the festal procession into the holy place. When the Psalm was written we cannot say, but it must have been long after the establishment of the Temple and its worship. If we accept any hypothesis at all that of Vaihinger is the more probable, that its author was one of the Levites banished by the usurper Athaliah. Ewald draws a picturesque sketch of King Jechoniah as its author. On his way as prisoner to Babylon he passes a night in the royal burg at Baneas; unable to sleep and scared by visions he rises and paces by moonlight the battlement of the castle, in full view of Hermon and the Jordan valley. It is a beautiful picture which Ewald sketches, but one may doubt if it would have occurred to him had he not read of Hamlet and the battlement of Elsinore. Whoever wrote the Psalm, it marks the highest attainment of the lyric art among the Shemitic people —some say among any people. The balance of the rhythm, the exquisite poise of the sentences, the minute and dainty touch in the setting of the words, give to the song an almost indescribable beauty. There lies hid under the general name, "Sons of Korah," an artist whose name should be inscribed on the roll of the world's literature as chief among the masters of pure form.

We have already seen that Psalm xliv. was one of those whose composition has been referred to the Maccabean era. Those who hold this view say it was written after the defeat of Joseph and Azariah by the Syrian mercenaries at the Valley of Jackals, near Jamnia. We have no right to refuse to consider this, as many have done, for the chief lament of the singer is over some defeat of the Jewish armies at this very place which he mentions by name in the nineteenth verse. Reasons we have before endeavored to make plain to you, create so strong a presumption against all Maccabean Psalms, that it seems preferable to refer its composition to the time of the invasion of Judah and the pillage of Jerusalem by the allied armies of the Philistines and Arabs in the reign of Jehoram, toward the close of the ninth century, or to the troubled years which immediately preceded the Exile. The Psalm is so impersonal in treatment that it offers no clue as to who the singer was. It is written in evil days, when the Jewish armies have just suffered a disastrous defeat. The city and Temple lie open to the enemy, and unless Jehovah personally help, utter ruin seems to stare his religion and country in the face. The song is elegiac in character, and does not lack strong touches, as the appeal in the twenty-third verse, "Awake! why slumberest Thou, O Jehovah?" but taking it for all in all, it is the weakest of the songs in the Korahite book. There runs through it also a vein of *quid pro quo* ethics, to say the least, foreign to the feelings of one who has learned that man in his very best estate can neither deserve nor lay claim to anything from Divinity.

Psalm xlv. is unique in more senses than one. As the inscription informs us, it is a marriage song or Epithalamium. Primarily, it is a personal and secular song, whose reception in the Psalter can only be explained by the later and secondary spiritual reference of it, which of course does not concern us now. It is a marriage song, written for the nuptials of some king of Judah with a princess of Tyrian descent. Some few have referred it to the marriage of Solomon with a daughter of Hiram. It seems more probable that the occasion of it was the festivities which accompanied Joram's bringing his Israelitic bride home to Jerusalem. Joram was married in the reign of his father Jehoshaphat, of which we spoke to you in the last lecture as not unlike the Solomonic in the splendor of the court and the prosperity of the state. It is true that Joram's vanity and headstrong obstinacy lost all his father had acquired, and involved his state in war and disaster, but he started life with the fairest promise, and amid the blessings of all his subjects. The Psalm is evidently composed for a choral, in which without difficulty the parts may be traced. Those may not have been far from right who suppose it to have been the song of greeting sung by the Temple choirs on the entry of the bridal pair into their capital. Who the poet was we do not know. From the paternal tone of his advice we may assume him to have been an aged man; from the way he speaks of the king some have imagined that he was his tutor, though this of course is no more than supposition. The song is admirably adapted to the purpose for which it was composed, and is by far the best choral in the Psalter. From its very nature we do not expect delicacy of work, such as we find in Psalm xlii., but though drawn with broader lines it does not lack, in brilliant color and the quick swing of the measure, many peculiar beauties of its own. For pureness and elevation of thought and style no marriage song has come down to us from classical antiquity comparable to it. Our King James translation is rarely less fortunate than in rendering this song, and the English reader gains an utterly different idea from that which the original means to convey.

Psalm xlvi. is in every way worthy to be placed side by side with Psalm xlii., and has been the inspiration of many of the choicest of modern religious lyrics, for example, Luther's " Ein' feste Burg ist unser Gott." The situation is not clear. It could have been equally well written on any of the half-dozen occasions to which its composition has been referred by the commentators or on none of them. A citizen of Jerusalem and a devoted adherent of its Temple worship expresses in verse, whose softness and delicate melody is almost elegiac, his confidence amid the thickening rumors of war, in the security and abiding prosperity of the city which Jehovah has chosen for His abode. It is one of the sweetest idyls of the Psalm collection, and one which men will read and enjoy so long as they take pleasure in religious song.

Psalm xlvii. has a much clearer historical situation. Toward the close of the reign of Jehoshaphat there was an incursion of the Bedouin hordes of Moabites and Ammonites from the East Jordan steppe, into the remarkable and confused particulars of whose invasion we cannot enter now. They advance within sight of Jerusalem, whose court and people are thrown into a panic. During the night a quarrel arises in the Bedouin camp over the division of the spoil, and they are utterly routed on the morrow by a force advancing on the flank to attack them. On the fourth day thereafter a festival is held in the valley of Beraka, and the people, led by the Sons of Korah, march to the music of trumpets and psalteries in triumphal procession back into the city. The historical allusions in this Psalm have persuaded many scholars of its composition for this occasion. Most admirably was the Psalm adapted for the martial music of such a procession. One hears reëchoed in the very words the shouts of the rejoicing multitude and the blare of the trumpets. Even were it not written for this occasion it must have been for some similar one. Ewald suggests that it was the triumphal processional with which the restored Temple was reëntered. The art of any such hymn written for music and popular song cannot be an elaborate one, and this song shows its origin and design on its face. It is now the New Year Psalm of the Synagogue, and through a curious mistake of some of the Greek fathers, not conversant with the original, it has come to be used in the Church on Ascension Day.[1]

Psalm xlviii. is not unlike Psalm xlvi.; its style however lacks the terseness and compactness of diction which lends such an irresistible attraction to the latter. We find in it many exquisite word-pictures, as in the second verse, where the poet paints Zion as beheld from the north, beautiful for situation, the joy of the whole earth. Did we not possess Psalm xlvi., it would be the masterpiece of this kind of song. It was composed at a time when Jerusalem had just been delivered from the danger of attack by an army of allied peoples—probably at the same period as Psalm xlvii.—the incursion of the allied Bedouin in the reign of Jehoshaphat. The author has outlived the danger, and returned in safety to the city he pours forth in

---

[1] In ver. 5 (of the English version) the going up of God was interpreted of the ascension of Christ. (T.)

these graceful measures his thanksgiving for its deliverance.

Psalm xlix. is a didactic poem, and we well know that not even the genius of Lucretius has succeeded in making a didactic poem readable. The didactic habit of mind is so incompatible with the poetic that either the thought lames the verse or the verse runs away with the thought. This Psalm is no exception to the rule, for the metre is sacrificed to the poet's wrestling to explain the enigma of life—the apparent success in this world of the evil and the vicious at the expense of the good. If any of you have read Shemitic literature extensively you will know that literary modesty is a quality of which even the best Shemitic writers seem utterly oblivious, but they should not be judged by Aryan standards, for this, as well as a lack of all high conception of the meaning of literary property, is a racial and not a personal defect. The author of this Psalm is a striking case in point. He begins like Elihu in the Book of Job by calling aloud on all the world, rich and poor, high and low, to attend while his mouth speaks wisdom and his mind unfolds the solution of it all. But he has no solution to offer which goes beyond the shallows of the current thought in his time. His conclusion penetrates no deeper into the mystery than that of the Ecclesiast—that all worldly good is, in its nature, a vain thing unworthy of pursuit, because it cannot save man from that death, which he says is to end all, and of aught beyond which the singer has no hope or intuition. A poem of such a nature is excluded from judgment by the canons of pure art, so it is much when we say for it that the poet has not utterly sacrificed form to thought as have the authors of some of the other didactic poems in our Psalter. Who the author was we do not know. His vocabulary and terminology are so scholastic that there may be some ground for the view of those who suppose him to have been a Levitical teacher in one of the Temple schools.

These seven songs are all that have been taken from the Korahite lyrics by the collector of our Second Book. For the sake of unity I will ask you to consider briefly in this connection rather than later, the three songs borrowed from the same collection by the compiler of the Third Book of our Psalter. Our review of them will then be complete.

The three songs in the Third Book, numbered in our version lxxxiv., lxxxv., lxxxvii., attributed by their inscriptions to the Korahite collection, show in form and measure unmistakable resemblances to the songs from the same collection we have just been examining.

Psalm lxxxiv. is to be placed side by side and compared with Psalm xlii., much in the same way that we have already compared Psalm xlviii. with Psalm xlvi. The poet is in exile. He is a Korahite who, in times past, stood as door-keeper in the house of his God; now detained by service among a heathen people, he longingly wishes himself one of the little company just setting out to appear at the feast in Zion— yea he would account himself happy were he even a bird that he might nestle near the shrine where are all his affections. The rhythm and sentiment are perfect. The author and situation have not been clearly settled. It may be from the first of the Judean captivities.

Psalm lxxxv., as the opening verse distinctly informs us, was written subsequent to the Exile: "when the captivity of Jacob had been brought back." It is a song full of thankfulness for the present deliverance and of hopeful augury for the opening era of the re-established state, when truth is to spring out of the ground and righteousness look down from heaven. The situation is clear. It was composed during one of the early returns of the exulants, probably the very first of these under Joshua and Zerubbabel. It does not lack resemblances in style to the later chapters of Isaiah.

The last of these Korahite songs, Psalm lxxxvii., is but a torso which has suffered more at the hands of its restorers and commentators than from the original mutilators. The author seems to be a patriotic burgher of Jerusalem who regards its citizenship as the highest distinction and privilege, and one which all the surrounding nations will speedily come to seek. The rhythm and thought both flow easily. It is usually referred to the time of exhilaration in Jerusalem which followed Sanherib's (Sennacherib's) defeat.

Thus we have run through all these songs of the Korahites which have been preserved to us in our Psalter. None of them seem earlier than the time of Jehoshaphat, none later than the close of the Exile. The art in almost all of them, though differing in degree, is perfect in its kind. It is a minute, elaborate and technical art, showing such influence of culture and the schools as renders it probable that all of them were composed by the Levitical singers, whose name the book from which they were taken bears. Their separate individuality offers a bar to the suggestion that all of them come from the same hand.

As to who the authors may have been we can in no case establish so much as a probability. But what need that matter? Does the question of authorship ever affect the beauty, the meaning, the influence of any song? Would not the nineteenth Psalm have the same force, the same inspiration for us and for all time, no matter by whom or in what century it was written? Does the forty-second Psalm lose one petal of its loveliness because from some obscure singer whose name the world has forgotten? Are these literary questions forever to be measured by the line and plummet of preconception? Theodoret was right when he told the Church of the fifth century that they attributed inspiration, not to Divinity, but to David—"We need not care," he says further, "who the authors were. The songs they bring us have been inspired for man's devotion until the end of time."

LECTURE VII.

In the three lectures which now remain to us in this present course, we shall, of necessity, be obliged to hasten over, or touch but cursorily upon, many points of interest in our Psalter, that we may have space to call your attention to other matters of importance, which are not accessible outside the technical literature, connected with the exposition of the original text. However, the literary problems arising in the study of the last four books are, to so great a degree the same as those we have already discussed at length in speaking of the collection and arrangement of the First Book, that we can, in general, assume the solution of them then suggested to hold good for all the books of the Psalter.

We were speaking to you in the last hour of the Second Book of our Psalter, which includes Psalms xlii–lxxii., and is a collection of thirty-one songs, made at a date somewhat later than that to which we are obliged to assign the First Book. We had the pleasure of examining the delicate and fragrant garland of song, gathered by the collector from the older "Lyrics of the Sons of Korah," which form the distinctive feature and characteristic beauty of the Second Book. Poetry of such dainty form and brilliant color is to be found nowhere else in Hebrew literature, and rarely, if at all, in any other literature. The English version preserves to us their thought, but the aroma of the delicate rhythm has been volatilized, and the subtle beauty of the word-painting has been blurred. One leaves them with reluctance to pass on to the other songs of the book.

The collector borrows one song, Psalm l., from the Book of Asaph, the leader of the Temple band at the time of David, but songs from the Book of Asaph form such a characteristic feature of the Third Book, where there are no less than twelve of them, that for the sake of unity of treatment, we will defer speaking of this Psalm until we come to take up the next book.

The collector also differs in method from the collector of the First Book, in making use of three anonymous songs, taken from no older collection of which we have any information. These are the songs numbered lxvi., lxvii., lxxi., in our version. Psalm xliii. of course cannot be reckoned among them, as it is no more than the final strophe of Psalm xlii., first made into a separate Psalm by a copyist's blunder; while Psalm lxxii., though without any superscription of authorship, is quite clearly referred to the "Davidic Book" by an editorial subscription, wrongly counted in our version as the final verse of the Psalm. The compilers are so minute and painstaking in the information they give us as to the songs of whose origin they have knowledge, that it is only fair to presume in the case of all the anonymous Psalms, not alone in this book, but also in the subsequent books, that they were themselves ignorant of the authorship and situation.

All peoples have their store of unwritten popular melody which, in the early time, when writing was an acquirement of a small learned or wealthy class, was far more extensive than we can gain any idea of from the habit of our own period, when the thought of the singer is no sooner articulate than it passes into the hands of the printer. The world has long since outgrown its ballad period, but at the time our Psalter was being collected, though on the verge of the days of book-making, the Hebrew people were still ballad-creators. We shall find later, in the Fifth Book, a number of ballads known as the "Songs of Degrees," which grew up among the people in their journeys, which thrice in the year they made from all over the land to the feasts in Jerusalem.

Of the origin of poetry among the Shemitic people, I hope, if time allow, to give you some account ere we close these lectures. Their ballad poetry, as that of every other people, was born silently and unobserved from the popular consciousness; grew up in the mouth of the people at their feasts and assemblies, was sung by their minstrels in ever varying form, until finally it received the literary fashion in which it has come down to the later time from some editor who caught and confined it in the fixed bounds of writing.

The ballad poetry of most peoples is of two kinds, either warlike or patriotic song, inspired by great victories and national deliverances, or the song of peaceful pastoral life—in both cases furnishing the student of history and of manners, with the truest picture of the life and surrounding of the people who sang them.

Israel was, as we shall hereafter see, from the earliest times in which we have record of them, a musical people, and one devoted to song. They celebrated their victories and feasts with dance and with song, many fragments of which are still preserved to us.

The motive of our Psalm collectors being purely religious, they have of course taken from this popular melody no songs save those fitted for use in the Temple worship. Most of them are religious ballads which grew up among the people during their feasts at the tabernacle or Temple. In regard to some of them it seems probable that they were first committed to writing by those who collected our Psalter.

But there is still another not insignificant source whence the anonymous Psalms have come. The service of the Temple was ceremonial and ritualistic, and accompanied through all its parts by an elaborate chanting of the various Temple choirs. For the purpose of this ceremonial Temple-song there were many pieces prepared by the priests, or even by the choir; arrangements of older melodies or original adaptations of familiar words of Scripture. As prepared for music and the use of the Temple choir, little stress would be laid on their arranger. When at a later time these arrangements were taken into our Temple Books most naturally they appeared anonymously. Their arranger or adapter may have been a member of the Temple choir whose individuality was sunk in that of the body to which he belonged, or in some cases he may have been, as the wont in our own day is, no more than some priest or Temple servant detailed for this special service.

When we come to examine the Fifth Book we shall find it largely made up of these songs which have been arranged for the use of the Temple-choir, whose rhythm fitted to music, whose meagre thought, whose reiteration of the same phrases, betray unmistakably to the student of the original their composition in the music-room of the Temple. Compare even in the English version Psalms like xix., or xlii., with musical compilations like Psalms cxxxvi., or cl., and you will, in some small degree, gain the same impression.

Now from one of these two sources, either from the popular religious lyrics, whose only author was the mouth of the people who sang them, or from the liturgical compilations for the Temple choir, the name of whose musical adapter was deemed of no moment, the great majority of our anonymous Psalms have come. It requires little knowledge either of poetry, or Hebrew style, to enable one quickly to discern to which class to refer any given song.

There then remains a very small residuum of anonymous songs whose personal allusions are so distinct, and of such a nature, as to lead us to refer them to some one or another of the poets or prophets who are known to us from the historical books. It is probable that these came to the Psalm collectors by verbal tradition, (of course in its simple line of transmission), for if they had come from any older book, the collectors' racial habit of mind and own personal scrupulousness of detail would have led them to make a note of it.

There can be little doubt that the collector's reason for giving us no inscription of authorship for these Psalms, was his inability to assure himself of the authorship with any certainty.

This whole question of anonymous Psalms, therefore, of which so much has been made, is really, as we have endeavored to present it, a very simple one, which need occasion no one the slightest difficulty. The doctors of the Talmud, with their fatal facility for finding mares' nests in every bush, have almost hopelessly muddled it, and strange to say, it is from them that most Christian scholars have learned, rather than from the study and comparison of the Psalms themselves. If you understand me then aright, you will see that the "anonymous Psalms" lack the inscription of authorship from so slightly mystical a reason as that their editor did not know who the author was. We fare no better in seeking now-a-days for the authorship from internal evidence. In regard to no one of them does the evidence create proof even strong enough to be called probable.

In our Second Book there are, as I before said, three of these anonymous Psalms.

The first of these, Psalm lxvi., is an admirable specimen of a liturgical song prepared for the Temple ritual. It seems to have been arranged for use in the service which accompanied the fulfillment of the vow in the Sanctuary. Despite the elevation of the monotheistic idea among the more enlightened minds in Israel, it was the common practice among the people, when in straits of any kind, to make a vow, conditioned upon alleviation or deliverance, of some offering or sacrifice to Jehovah at His shrine. We learn that no small part of the duties of the priests was the reception and proper offering of these vowed sacrifices. For this service the song has been prepared. It is divided into two parts—verses 1–12, the responsive chant of the Temple choirs, with which the service was introduced; 13–20, the chant of the officiating priest as he took from the worshipper his vowed offering, and presented it to Jehovah. The parts may be distinguished without difficulty, both from their style and from their allusions. As in most of the liturgical Psalms, the arranger has drawn on older songs which he has adapted for use in the particular ceremony he had in view. Such an arrangement for constant use can scarcely be said to have an historical situation; whoever the arranger may have been, he was soon forgotten.

Psalm lxvii. is an exquisite bit of popular lyric. It is a harvest home song of thanksgiving, sung by the reapers as they followed from the field the last of their wains, groaning under the heavily laden bounty of nature—or equally well, a ballad of the harvest feast, when the fruits of the earth had been garnered, and the people were gathered for rejoicing at the shrine in Shiloh. It is an old song preserved for generations in the mouth of the people, and doubtless all knowledge of its authorship or origin had been lost.

Psalm lxxi. has too personal a stamp to be referred either to the liturgic songs of the Temple, or to the popular impersonal melody of the people. The singer is an old man who has passed a troubled and varied life; now just on the verge of the grave, he is exposed to some new danger, from which he begs to be delivered. His song is neither original nor forcible. It is simply an anthology of bits from older psalms pieced together with small art, and scarce any regard to connection or sequence of thought. The breadth of style, the lack of grasp, the prosaic thought of such part of it as is original, have led some over-acute critics to refer it to Jeremiah, they further laying stress on the anthological method as being characteristic of the Jeremianic style.

Jeremiah certainly is one of the least original or acute of the Hebrew prophets whose writings have come down to us. His thought flows sluggishly and prosaically. He lacks all the power which Isaiah in so marked a degree possesses, to illumine what he says with the touch of style. His reading has surfeited him; he has none of the mystic alembic called genius to fuse it in the crucible of his mind, into new forms. His writings show no sustained literary effort, and are destitute of clear and vigorous thought. He expresses himself so largely not only in the ideas but in the very words of the books he has read, that he may, with justice, be called an anthologist. If ever you take up a critical study of Jeremiah you will find many scholars using a much harder word of him, and that is plagiarism. But it is unjust, for plagiarism implies a moral obliquity in the use of the material of another, which is incompatible with what we know of Jeremiah's character. We can simply say, his style was an unhappy one, from whose trammels his inspiration did not free him.

Undoubtedly the style and method of the author of our Psalm resemble Jeremiah's, but that is surely slight ground on which to base proof of Jeremianic authorship. Could no one else in Judea have had a nerveless style, freely interlarded with quotation, save Jeremiah? Is it not probable if it had come from a man whose writings were collected with such pious care by his pupils as were Jeremiah's, that we should have had some note or recollection of the author preserved? We know, of surety, no more of the authorship than did the post-exilic editor who gave it a place in his song collection.

The editors of the early Greek translation characteristically display their ignorance by attributing this Psalm to the Rechabites, a Bedouin clan descended from the Kenites, one of the Arab peoples allied with Israel in their march through the desert, who seem to have entered Palestine with them, and to have dwelt in friendship with them there.

The Rechabites are known to us from the time when they sought temporary refuge behind the walls of Jerusalem, from the advance of the Chaldean armies. Jeremiah holds up their temperance—a virtue common from the earliest times among the Bedouin Shemites, but gradually shading out in the ratio of their increasing civilization, as an example to his own dissolute[1] fellow-citizens. It has occurred to me that the Greek translator, casting about for some author, which he feels in duty bound to find for every Psalm, and noticing in our Psalm a style not unlike that of Jeremiah, has, from their connection with him, been led to pitch upon the Rechabites, than which no more unfortunate reference could be made. The song must have been written by some one intimately acquainted with the older Psalms, and there is not a trace in it

---

[1] Jeremiah (Jer. xxxv.) holds up the Rechabites as an example not of temperance, but of obedience to paternal commands, in order to rebuke his fellow-citizens, not for dissoluteness, but for disobedience to the commands of Jehovah. (T.)

of the clear air, and glinting sand of the desert, which are always reflected in the songs of the Bedouin.

We consequently see the value, or rather, valuelessness of these historical notices found in the Septuagint with all the anonymous Psalms.

The collector of our Second Book also makes a supplementary draft of eighteen songs, on the older Davidic Temple Book, which bears all the marks of a supplemental loan. The collector of the First Book had already culled the choicest lyrics of the older collection. There are none of the Davidic songs in this Second Book of our Psalter, which, for beauty of measure, or depth of thought, can be compared with those in the First Book.

The most interesting of the Davidic Songs in the Second Book is the first of them, numbered in our version Psalm li.

Metrically it cannot be called so strong a poem as many others of the master. It is the bitter wail of a heart-broken man, athwart whose life a curse more fatal than ever the old Greek tragedy had painted was beginning to darken. Incest, fratricide, and rebellion in his own family, civil war among his people, and expulsion from his capital was the cup which avenging justice was pressing to his unwilling lips, and of which he was obliged to drain the last dregs. Scholars have, without reason, impugned the accuracy of the editor's note as to the origin of this song.

Psalm liii., we have already seen, is precisely the same song as Psalm xiv., though taken from a later and an imperfect manuscript, in regard to which we have spoken sufficiently in a former lecture.

Psalm lviii. is a satirical song on the unjust judges of the people. The figures come trooping so rapidly into the poet's imagination, that the outline of one is scarcely filled out before he begins another. The poem is, therefore, a very difficult one, and in places our English renders it unfortunately.

In the tenth verse we find one of those touches of the poet which betray a civilization and ethical code far different from our own. If the teaching of our highest ethical and religious culture be that it is far nobler to forgive than to avenge an injury, better to suffer than to do wrong, there can be no excuse for the vindictive passages in the Psalms, and they have never been defended save by a special pleading, unworthy of the scholarship and the enlightened morals of its authors. Israel's mission to the world was simply a religious one, to keep alive the spark of monotheistic revelation, which in a new era was to be kindled into a flame. Their civilization and moral codes were neither better nor worse than those of the surrounding peoples. We do not excuse their polygamy; why should we seek to palliate their barbarous war-code? Jael's treacherous slaughter of her ally; Jephthah's sacrifice of his virgin daughter—they mark a civilization which the world has outgrown, and to which none of us would willingly return. We justly feel nothing but reprobation for David's conduct toward the conquered Ammonites, in tearing them asunder under his saws and harrows of iron. We shudder at the habit of mind which could allow him with his dying breath to curse his enemies, and leave as a parting injunction upon his son, "to bring down their hoary hairs in blood into the grave." It is not an ideal which the civilized world now regards as imitable.

What I said of the literary style of the Hebrew writers, is equally true of their ethical codes. As little as inspiration changes a man's style, does it raise him beyond the thinking of the time in which he lives.

In David's time revenge upon personal or national enemies was not regarded as wrong. He was giving expression to what was the natural feeling of himself and his people, in praying that their feet might be dipped in the blood of their enemies, and the tongues of their dogs might lap it up. The make-up of the Shemitic character was altogether unique. With great tenderness to their own tribe or family, and an acutely-strung religious sensibility, there was, in dealing with others, an utter lack of many of those moral standards which, to the Aryan mind, seem primary and fundamental. As a matter of course, their habit of mind is reflected in their literature, and curses similar to that on Babylon, in Psalm cxxxvii., where the singer pronounces him happy who will take their infants and dash them against the stones, are no novelty to any one conversant with the literature of the other Shemitic peoples.

The question of the vindictive Psalms is one of the most famous ones in the theological study of the Old Testament Scripture, which, of course, is a side with which, in this place, we are not concerned. But even in the literary study of the Psalter we must make some explanation of them, and the most satisfactory seems to be, that they are the natural expression of a civilization and ethical culture alien to our own. If our standards of morals be of any value, it was a civilization consciously lower than that of the present, and for which, from our standpoint of doing as we would wish to be done by, there can be no palliation. Bear in mind that it is the fidelity with which the Hebrew writings preserve the acts and words of its heroes, suppressing nothing and palliating nothing, which furnishes, more than the most ingenious plea of apologists, a convincing defence against the searching attacks on its credibility and authenticity by many of the most acute scholars. If inspired men have done things which are wrong, says Tholuck, why may they not have uttered words which were selfish, or passionate, or resentful? The Psalms present us with an almost Shaksperean picture of the moral workings in the hearts of their authors. He is blind who cannot see in them the touch of nature which doth make the whole world kin.

Psalm lxv. is a harvest-song from the Davidic Book. Scholars, who imagine they can give us year and day for each Psalm, have figured this so closely that they tell us it was composed for the Harvest Feast — Feast of Pentecost — held June 6, B. C. 707. All we can say is, that we do not know it was not.

Psalm lxviii. is, beyond dispute, the most difficult of the Psalms; perhaps, taking it all in all, the most obscure passage of the Hebrew Scripture. It is apparently a war song—in style not unlike the Song of Deborah—sung by a victorious procession, marching in triumph into Jerusalem. In its interpretation, probably no two scholars have ever agreed. The vocabulary is extremely recondite, and in many places the text has been so injured, that one is baffled in his search for sense or connection.

Psalm lxx., as I showed in another connection, is a

fragment of the older Psalm xl., reshaped for certain liturgical uses.

Psalm lxxii., of which I have also spoken, was, as our English version rightly has it, composed "for," and not "by," Solomon.

Thus we have run through all the more noteworthy songs of the Second Book. As to their arrangement we may remark, as we did in reference to the First Book, that if the collector had any principle of arrangement, it is no longer discoverable.

The collection of the Second Book is referred by many to Nehemiah. Though we have no sure information, there is an old tradition of this, and it is not improbable that it is correct.

Nehemiah was a prince of the Davidic lineage. He had been educated at the Persian court, of which, in the days of its greatest splendor, he was a prominent official. From the nature of his position he must have been a man of wealth and culture. History further discloses him to us as a man of considerable administrative ability, and of great force of character. His story is told in the book, which, not written by him, bears his name as its hero.

But there is another side of his story equally true, which we must understand ere we can comprehend Nehemiah's mission to his people in the right light. The power of Persia had received a staggering blow, in the victories gained over it by the Greeks. Not long before this time the great king was obliged to accept humiliating treaties both from the Greeks and Egyptians. Milman reports that among the conditions of the treaty with the Greeks was a surrender of all the maritime towns, and a stipulation that no Persian troops were to approach nearer than three days march from the seaboard. Jerusalem, being about this remove from the sea, became a post of great importance, to be occupied and fortified, if possible, by the people themselves without any such display of Persian force as would alarm their enemies.

Again, the people of Palestine had begun to grow restive, imagining in this time of disaster they saw their opportunity for shaking off the Persian yoke. It was essential for the sake of order, that the Jews be gained over to the Persian cause. The Persian court acted with wisdom in sending as a secret commissioner, for that his mission was secret is shown by the stealth with which he makes his journey, an official of the court on whose fidelity they placed reliance, and yet one whose race and royal descent would gain him acceptance with the Jews, who, even in their misfortune, remained obstinately national. Nehemiah arrives in Jerusalem in the spring of 444 B. C., seventy-two years after the completion of the Temple, almost a century after the first return under Joshua and Zerubbabel, and fourteen years later than the arrival of Ezra, who still survived. Of Nehemiah's civil administration, in which he deserved well both of his king and compatriots, we can not speak now. He fortified Jerusalem with a skill which indicates a knowledge of engineering, and then secured a sufficient garrison to hold it, by a levy on the people of the outlying villages. Despite great opposition among the upper classes, he gains the people for the Persian cause, to which they remain loyal until its power was shattered in the next century by Alexander's spearmen in the battle of Issus. But even as the agent of the king, he does not forget his nationality. He interests himself deeply in the welfare of his people, and introduces many reforms both in their worship and administration, which his position gives him authority to carry through.

Jewish tradition reports him to have made a collection of hymns for the Temple service. If there be any truth in the tradition at all, it probably refers to his collection of the Second Book of our Psalter, and also the Third, which we shall presently see is but a supplement to the Second. Bred in the atmosphere of a foreign court, Nehemiah's acquaintance with the literature of his country would be largely of the literary and æsthetic sort, and it is the hand of an editor working with a literary instinct, which we discern in the collection of the Second and Third Books.

We can understand why, at the time of the return under Joshua a century earlier, the collector of the First Book, some priest or Levite, whose memory might well extend back to the former Temple, drew his material alone from the "Davidic Temple Book," which use had made sacred to him.

We can equally well understand how a man of Nehemiah's training, if he be indeed the collector, would pass beyond the old service-books, and gather from all sources, those songs whose beauty of thought or rhythm had attracted him. Whoever the collector be, he has enriched the world's imagination in preserving such gems from the "Songs of the Sons of Korah."

The Third Book is a much shorter one than the Second, and includes the eighteen songs numbered in our version Psalms lxxiii.–lxxxix. It was apparently collected by the same hand as the Second Book, and bears evidence of being a collection supplementary to it.

It contains a small remainder of the Korahite songs, numbered in our version Psalms lxxxiv., lxxxv., lxxxvii., of which we spoke in the last hour.

The only Psalm taken by the collector from the Davidic Book is the fourteenth in the book, or Psalm lxxxvi., as we number in our King James. It is a purely liturgical song, a cento made up of fragments from older Psalms, which need not detain our attention.

The inscription of the last song, Psalm lxxxix., attributes its authorship to Ethan the Ezrahite, of the tribe of Judah, one of the wise men whose sayings were proverbial in the time of Solomon, not to be confounded with a Levite of the same name, who was one of the leaders of the Temple orchestra. The song is composed in an evil time for the Jewish State. The singer calls to mind the glorious promises made to the Davidic house, and in words scarce articulate through sobs, he pleads their non-fulfilment before Jehovah. The covenant of God with His people seems void; the land is over-run with enemies; Jerusalem has been captured; the throne of David has been cast to the ground, and the youthful king who sat upon it has been shamefully entreated. If there be any credence to be placed in the inscription of authorship to a contemporary of Solomon, there is but one situation to which the song can be referred, the invasion of Judea by the Egyptian army under Shishak, in the early years of the reign of Rehoboam.

Shashang, called in the Bible Shishak, first of the twenty-second Egyptian dynasty, was the son of an

Assyrian captain, who met his death in Abydos, and who set up a dynasty at Bubastis, in the Lower Nile country, under circumstances which do not concern us now.

Jeroboam, who in the closing years of Solomon's reign, had become the centre for the wide-spread disaffection with the exactions of that sovereign, obliged to fly for his life, took refuge with and was received with friendliness by the Egyptian king. On Solomon's death it was by Shashang's aid that Jeroboam was helped to the throne of Ephraim, and it was, no doubt, at the suggestion of his former guest, who held the Jewish armies in check on the north, that Shashang was moved to the invasion which proved so disastrous to Judah.

The Hebrew chroniclers, loth to record the shame of their people, and the utter break-up of the Solomonic kingdom within less than a generation after his death, hasten over their recital of the invasion with a few lines. But in the rainless air of Egypt has been preserved for thirty centuries the inscription carved on his return by King Shashang as a memorial of thanksgiving for the victory granted him by his divine patron, Amen of Thebes, the clear decipherment of which by Champollion, did more than any thing else to accredit the study of the hieroglyphs. In the south wall of the temple at Karnak the spectator may still behold in colors almost as fresh as the day on which they were painted, the colossal shape of the Egyptian sovereign, dealing heavy blows with his victorious war-mace on the troops of captive Jews whom he drives before him. Around him are a series of cartouches illustrative of the cities and towns he has conquered. Near the centre is one representing Jerusalem in which is the figure of a young man, led a captive, and beneath him is the inscription Judhmelek—The King of Judah. It is probably the unfortunate Rehoboam. We could seek no more striking confirmation of the situation for the song of the now aged Ethan, who pours out in this mournful rhythm the whole story of national ruin, disaster and disgrace.

Macaulay said if we want the truth as to any time we must seek for it in the contemporaneous songs and ballads, rather than in the narrations of subsequent annalists. I think you perceive, that in this Psalm, we gain a fuller idea of the crushing defeat of Rehoboam, than we could do from the meagre notices in the historical annals of the Kings and Chronicles.

Psalm lxxxviii. is pitched on the lowest and most hopelessly mournful key of any of the Psalms. The situation is a purely personal one. The singer represents himself as a man afflicted with leprosy, which makes him an abomination and shuts him off from all communication with his kind. It has come to him through no fault of his own, but by inheritance; from his youth up he can remember nothing but weary and loathsome years of pain. Manifestly nothing of the sort would be applicable to the reputed author, Heman, the Ezrahite, who, as the historical books inform us, was one of the nobles of the Solomonic court. The idea, and very words as well, remind us so forcibly of Job, that if we accept Heman's authorship, against which no valid ground can be urged, we shall do better to explain the song as an adaptation or recollection from the Book of Job. The story of Job was a very popular one in the time of Solomon, when it was probably translated into Hebrew, and received the literary form in which we now have it.

But most deserving of attention, and most characteristic of the Third Book, are the eleven Psalms the editor has borrowed from the older "Songs of Asaph." We have, however, a far different judgment to pass on their art and style than that of the last hour on the cultured and delicate lyrics of the Korahites.

Poetry is the artistic expression of the imagination through language; differing thus from music, which is the expression of the imagination through sound, as sculpture through form, painting through color, and so on around the circle of the arts.

This being so, our present conception of poetry, as coincident with rhythm, is a faulty one. In the poetry of many peoples, and markedly in that of the Shemitic people, there is no trace of formal rhythm such as we understand by the term. I doubt if there is a single song in the Psalter, which, in the original, could be made to rhyme. The only rhythm in Hebrew poetry is rhythmical thought, and what I mean by this you may perchance understand if you are acquainted, in contemporaneous English literature, with the so-called prose of Ruskin or Pater, which you are doubtless aware has more claim to be regarded as poetry than much of our so-called verse.

From the material with which it deals, poetry is commonly divided into Lyric and Epic.

Lyric poetry is a subjective art, in which the poet gives expression alone to the pictures painted in his imagination by his personal passion or emotion.

Epic poetry is an objective art, in which the poet gives expression to the shapes into which his imagination has cast the facts of the external world coming into contact with it.

Of lyric poetry, we have already met with examples in our study of the Psalter: of epic poetry we shall speak in a moment.

Now these Songs of Asaph belong to neither of these well recognized classes of poetry, but to another and less commonly recognized one called didactic poetry.

Didactic Poetry is commonly defined as that in which the poet primarily proposes to himself teaching of some kind, either ethical, or religious, or literary. If the poet merely gives expression to his mental processes as they reflect themselves in his imagination, with no object in view beyond their utterance, of course it is poetry, just as much as the similar expression of his passion or emotion. But if he consciously propose to himself as a primary object, either teaching or persuasion of any kind, there come into play such intellectual processes as to exclude the product from the category of poetry. So at least critics have quibbled and split hairs over the right of didactic poetry to a place among the arts. Probably the truth is that the intellectual element involved in a didactic poem, is always at the expense of the imaginative—the better the teaching, the poorer, of necessity, is the poetry. And yet, from the earliest times men seem to have had an irresistible impulse toward committing their thinking and teaching to the one vehicle least fitted to convey it. Witness "The Theogony" of Hesiod, "The Georgics" of Virgil, the "De Natura Rerum" of Lucretius; or, coming to our own literature, the unreadable mass of verse from the morally didactic school so popular at the beginning of this century, whose best representative is Cowper's Task.

Under this same class of didactic poetry these Songs of Asaph are all to be placed; but before we can estimate aright their personal peculiarities we must see who Asaph was.

Asaph was one of the first figures pitched upon for attack by the Leyden school, who, to their own satisfaction, made short work of him, leaving not even the wrack of his name behind. My opinion of their methods, which involve more difficulties than those they solve, I have already alluded to, and will not revert to now.

Asaph was born not far from the year 1050 B. C., of a Levitical family who lived in a country village of the upland of Ephraim. Through all his poetry there runs a vein of tender feeling for the home of his childhood, and one of the most mournful of our Psalms is his lament over Ephraim's revolt, which, as an old man, he had lived to behold and grieve over. His favorite figures of a shepherd and the sheep, which are found in almost all these songs, and are reiterated and dwelt on by him as by no other singer in our Psalter, are perhaps recollections of his boyish days when he himself followed the flock.

As a young man he seems to have entered one of the prophetical schools of Samuel—a master whose memory he revered, and whose influence is very apparent in his poetry. It was here, doubtless, that his mind received that didactic cast which ever after remained so characteristic of it, and from his stay in this school came the appellation of "seer" or prophet, by which he was commonly known.

The teaching of these schools was accompanied by music, in which the young man—for he must have been then a very young man to have lived until the revolt of Ephraim—so excelled as to attract the attention of David, who appointed him second band-master in the Temple orchestra. There is an evident confusion in the chronicler's mind as to whether Heman or Asaph was the leader of the Temple band, which finds its solution in the probable fact that Heman was the real leader, while Asaph was the more prominent musician of the two.

His favorite instrument, with which he led the band, and on which he is expressly spoken of as a solo performer, was the cymbals, which, quite remarkably, in Egypt, whence Israel borrowed their musical instruments, were only allowed to be used in sacred music.

He died in the reign of Rehoboam, and left a numerous family, who seem to have retained as well their ancestor's cast of mind as his musical ability.

His descendants are spoken of as in the orchestra of the Temple at the time of Jehoshaphat, and later again, in the reign of Hezekiah; one hundred and forty-eight of them return from the Exile with Joshua, and receive the same position in the restored Temple.

We learn from the inscriptions of these Psalms that Asaph was a poet. From the Psalms themselves, we learn, if I may say so, that he was a man of decided poetic genius, who endeavored to set forth in poetry, his extensive readings, and ideas of a kind which, in their nature, are incapable of a suitable treatment in it. The perceptible struggle in his verse between the intellect and the imagination is a painful one; it renders it obscure to us, as, no doubt, it must also have been to his contemporaries. In reading him it always occurs to me that he was a man of the same order of mind as Robert Browning.

All the poems which bear his name cannot, however, have been his personal composition, as some of them contain clear allusions to events which could not have occurred until long after his time. It is only fair to presume that there was in his family a book bearing his name, and containing his poems, and that to this, little by little, there were added other poems of the same manner. We have already seen that this was so in the case of the Davidic Book, and it strikingly approves itself as so here, by the statement in Chronicles, that when the commission of Hezekiah collected the "Songs of David," they also collected "the Writings of Asaph." This doubtless was the "Book of Asaph," from which the collector of the Second and Third Books has taken the songs which appear in our Psalter.

The only one of these Asaphian Songs found in the Second Book is Psalm l., the most vigorous of them all in thought and expression, seemingly pointing to the collector of the Second Book's having had the first selection of them, somewhat in the way that the compiler of the First Book had of the Davidic collection, or the compiler of the Second Book of the "Songs of Korah." The poet represents in a grand theophany, like that of old on Sinai, Jehovah appearing, and calling His people before Him to make clear to them the real meaning of His law, which had become to them no more than a ceremonial observance. He rises to an ethical height in his apprehension of the meaning of religion, as an ordering aright of one's life before God, which is far beyond his time. His teaching that sacrifice is a vain thing, seems almost an echo of the saying of his master, "that to obey is better than sacrifice, and to hearken, than the fat of rams."

The poet is a man of elevated and lucid thought, of clear and perspicuous expression. There can be no convincing ground urged against the author's being Asaph himself, nor do I see the cogency of the evidence which has led most scholars to refer its composition to the reign of Josiah.

It is, however, from the Third Book, that we gain our best idea of the measure and manner of Asaph's genius, for over half of this book is composed of Asaphian songs, which we will briefly run through.

The first of them is Psalm lxxiii., in which the poet is struggling with the problem which seemed for the ancient Hebrews the hardest to solve—how, if there be a divine government of men, can the wicked be allowed to prosper at the expense of the righteous? So troubled is he with the evil and oppression he sees all around him, that he is about giving up all belief in a moral order of the world. Thinking it over he at length enters into the sanctuary of God, *i. e.*, he penetrates into the hidden thought of the divine government and perceives that in the unhappy end of all evil doers lies the solution of the mystery. The thought is sustainedly elevated, and hovers on the very edge of an intuition of a conscious future immortality, which the singer, even if he were able to grasp, seems unable to formulate. It is among the strongest of these poems. The author and situation, from the very nature of the poem, are not clear.

The next is Psalm lxxiv. In studying the question of the Maccabean Psalms, we have examined this Psalm sufficiently. We then saw there was a possibility that Psalms lxxiv. and lxxix. came from that period. If you are further interested in the question of their origin you will find the reasons, pro and contra, ably discussed and weighed, from the conservative side, by Delitzsch in his Commentary on the Psalms—at the best in the last German edition.

Psalm lxxv. is a prophetic vision of God's judgments on the heathen, etched in broad light and shade by the lyric burin. The Septuagint is probably correct in referring it to the judgment against the Assyrian; the style and allusions as well are very similar to the burdens against Assyria in the prophetic writings. As a specimen of the interpretation of the newer school, whose standard is the subjective one of taste, I may mention Hitzig's reference to this as the song sung by Judas Maccabeus, when he conquered Apollonius. He actually represents him dancing around his fallen foe, whose head he has just hewn off, singing, " All the horns of the wicked will I cut off, but the horns of the righteous shall be exalted."

Psalm lxxvi. is poetically the most noteworthy of

the Songs of Asaph. The expression is graceful, and the cadence melodious. The singer having no ethical problem to work out, has devoted more attention to the form of the poem, but is unable entirely to free himself from the didactic habit, which alone prevents the song from being ranked among the very best of the Psalter. The reference in it to the stout-hearted who, "with their chariots and horses, have been cast into a deep sleep," points unmistakably to the destruction of the host of Sanherib (Sennacherib) and gives us the situation of the poem.

In Psalm lxxvii. the poet is in despair over some national calamity—many imagine the revolt of the ten tribes—from which he struggles free by calling to mind the days of old, and Jehovah's former dealings with His people, as an augury for future good. The Psalm ends abruptly without completion, and in the midst of a thought. Whether this be a flaw in the manuscript, or the song was left incomplete by its author, we do not know. The song is of chief interest, as having furnished Habakkuk with the idea of the glowing theophany in the last chapter of his prophecy, as a comparison will show you. It is, consequently, a very old song.[1]

Psalm lxxviii., with its seventy-two verses, is the

---

[1] The date of the prophecy of Habakkuk is about B. C. 610. (T.)

longest of the Songs of Asaph, and is one of the most interesting specimens of Hebrew epic poetry.

Epic poetry, as I scarcely need repeat, after what I said a moment ago, is simply narrative poetry, in which the singer clothes with verse the facts or objects, either real or imagined, of the external world which surround him, or of which he has learned from history. In a word, it is objective poetry, differing thus from lyric or subjective poetry in which the artist throws on his canvas only the pictures of the imagination, arising from the subjective passion or emotion of the moment, and which is purely the expression of personal excitement or exaltation. There is no inherent reason why an epic should not be written on the events and persons of one's own daily life. The poetic faculty refuses readily to grasp these as too familiar and commonplace—there is no play for fancy in their description, so the more usual sphere of the epic has been incidents and personages remote enough, either in time or place, for a halo of romance to have formed around them, on which the imagination has room to work. So it is that among every people, its early and heroic age is the favorite field of the epic poem. We need search no further for an illustration than our own land and time. We might with reason hope for an epic on the Pilgrim Fathers, or the early colonists. In fact, I do not know but that our common conception of them is in a measure epical, but I greatly doubt whether we can expect an epic on our own day, until the lapse of a couple of centuries has obliterated our failings, and projected our virtues into mythical outline.

The epic, you further know, may have its rise among the people, from the recollections which cluster around some eponymous hero, or national epoch; such are the Iliad, the Nibelungen, the Cid, or our own Arthurian Cycle. Or it may be the original product of some poetic artist, whose imagination has cast into new shape the materials of history and tradition; such are Virgil's "Æneid," Camoen's " Lusiad," or Tasso's " Jerusalem Delivered."

It has, of late, become a common phrase, in all our histories of literature, that the Shemitic mind is utterly destitute of the creative and fictile faculty, essential to the composition of an epic, and that nowhere in Shemitic literature is an epic to be found. It is one of the astounding statements for which the history of literature is indebted to M. Renan, which, as everything he writes, is presented by him with such grace of style, and apparent fairness, that a layman is first charmed, and then persuaded.

One would find it difficult, however, to exclude this Psalm from the epic cycle, under any definition of it which could be given. The poet, to whom the history of his people is familiar, reproduces it in an epic song which only fails of being a great one from his fatal didactic habit, which always clips his wings when about to make his highest flight. The truth is that there is not less epic poetry among the Shemitic than other peoples. You need go no further than our Psalter to find no less than a dozen epic songs. Though the Shemitic habit of mind was predisposed to lyric song, in which it has produced the world's masterpieces, there was nothing in it which unfitted it for epic poetry, as we could abundantly show from the literature of each of its peoples, were we not already at the closing of the hour.

Psalm lxxx. contains the beautiful figure of Israel as the goodly vine, of old transplanted from Egypt, now broken and wasted, which the poet probably intends as a symbol of the dissensions which had arisen between Ephraim and Judah. The cadence is touchingly soft and elegiac.

Psalm lxxxi. is, one might almost say, a homily composed, as it distinctly says, for one of the feasts; there is some doubt whether this was the spring feast of the Passover or the autumn one of Tabernacles.

Psalm lxxxii. was the regular Tuesday Psalm in the Temple. This we surely know, for we have still preserved in the Talmud the rubrics in which the

Psalms were arranged for daily, weekly and monthly use in the service.

Psalm lxxxiii. is the last of the eleven "Songs of Asaph" in this book. It is the petition of some singer for the deliverance of his people from a league of East-Jordan folk which is threatening them. The situation is clear, as in the time of Jehoshaphat, of which I spoke to you, in connection with Psalm xlviii. Possibly the author may have been Jahaziel, of the sons of Asaph, whose speech in the council of war at this time turned the tide, and lent new courage to the army which was about to fly. There are beside several likenesses of style between this Psalm and the speech of Jahaziel, reported somewhat at length in Chronicles, which would justify this conclusion.

Our review of the songs taken into our Psalter from the Asaphite Book is now complete. The general sketch of their literary peculiarities was given as we began our review, and we have now nothing further to add to it.

The Collector of this Third Book, we have seen, was, probably, the same as of the Second, to which it seems to be supplemental. Of his method we spoke sufficiently when reviewing the Second Book. In the next hour we will pass on to consider the Fourth and Fifth Books of our Psalter, and the new problems which arise in connection with them.

The source of all true poetry must be the human imagination, and the singer who gives utterance to the verse is but the creature of his age. Of no singers is this truer than of those whose songs are preserved in our Psalm Book. They are intensely national, narrowly local and personal, yet through their verse there runs a silver thread of something which binds it to the highest religious consciousness of the most civilized nations of the earth. The heart of man is, and ever will be, swayed by the songs of the Hebrews as by none other.

LECTURE VIII.

In the last lecture, we had the pleasure of examining together some of the many questions of interest arising in connection with the Second and Third Books of our Psalter. We found at every point inviting vistas, whose beauty was suggestive of delightful and repaying study, but, in the scant space of the hour, we could take no more than a glance down each of them.

I often fear you may regard my treatment of the Psalms as rather a flitting from flower to flower of its poesy, but, in the lectures of which this brief course has been made up, it has been infeasible to do more than barely touch upon the more noteworthy Psalms, and some few of the distinctive features of their literary method and poetic art.

The latest French writer on æsthetics, M. Véron, tells us that the most favorable conditions for active personal receptivity and assimilation are found in ruins, vanishing lines, unfinished work; it is in leaving to his reader or auditor an opportunity to fill up and complete at will all detail of the sketch, that the literary artist shows his power. I may at least, therefore, have the satisfaction of knowing that these lectures, imperfect as they are, are in accord with both the spirit and letter of this newest canon of æsthetics.

At the closing of the hour, we were discussing the artistic genius of Asaph, which we saw was of the didactic order. We further saw that didactic poetry, or that in which the artist proposes to himself to interpret thought, and to appeal to the intellect, is, by its very nature, excluded from the highest poetry, which is a creation of the imagination. Asaph was an artist of genius, and a man of clear and lofty thought. In discussing the limitations of his art, we had occasion to refer to the various forms of poetry as they appear among the Shemitic people. In the closing moments of the hour we were endeavoring to show the falsity of the view, now so generally obtaining in all histories of culture, that Shemitic literature is destitute of the epic song.

Hand in hand with this view, of the barrenness in the Shemitic mind of that objectivity and fictile skill essential to the epic, is the other view, which then I did not have time to mention, of its lack of all dramatic power. Both are outgrowths of the brilliant misapprehension of M. Renan as to the genius of the Shemitic race. For proof of the absence of the drama in Shemitic literature he has naught to urge, save a half dozen epigrams sparkling with the style of which he is so consummate a master, and a few stories of the failure of French opera companies in Algiers and Beyrout, clever enough as after dinner talk, but little to the purpose in a literary investigation which lays claim to be serious. One almost despairs of any advance in the comparative study of the world's literature and art, when theories like this, unripe even in their author's brain, only need utterance to be accepted. As a matter of fact, we have preserved, even in the sacred literature of the Jews, the oldest and perhaps most characteristic dramatic poetry which has come down to us from antiquity.

Drama is the representation, by a poetic artist, of the action or conversation of individuals other than himself. They may or may not be purely the creatures of his imagination. As through them alone the movement of the story, or the development of the plot is to be gathered, it is essential to a perfect dramatic art that the artist remain in the background. If the figures that move before us express aught which, not arising naturally from their surrounding, betrays the artist's inspiration of them, the effect of the art is destroyed. There are therefore essential to the dramatic artist two qualities, creative imagination, and the power of impersonal representation of action.

Drama is the highest form of the poetic art, borrowing from the epic its material, from the lyric its method, and possessing, as a subtle power fusing the two, a keen insight into the development of character in different measure.

It is a mistaken conception of dramatic art which makes it coincident with scenic effect; this latter is but a spur to the imagination, and has never obtained save among peoples destitute of personal dramatic power, for a background suggestive of what the artist or actor could not convey. I have no lance to break with the present art-theories running counter to this view, but I cannot but regard them as insufficient, because gained from an observation of the artistic phenomena peculiar to a single family of our race. Whatever the failings of the Shemitic racial habit may be—and that they are numerous and far-reaching enough to place them on a perceptibly lower plane than the Indo-European, we have seen to abundance in the progress of these lectures—we cannot, however, deny them the possession of a more highly developed dramatic power than any other people.

Art, to have its highest effect, must be personal.

It is through human feature, human voice and human gesture, that it can alone exercise its perfect working. All else is subsidiary and a help to this. Go into any coffee-house in the Levant, and observe the Arab story-teller, whose only property is the ragged mat he sits upon, whose only company the myriad shapes which people his brain, as he relates the romance of Antar, that story of wonder without beginning or end. Watch the subtle facial expression, the modulation of his voice toned to a fineness incredible to an occidental, the skilful gesture which interprets the thought even to one ignorant of the speech, and you will witness a pure dramatic effect which it would be impossible for the most skilled European company, even with the property of Baireuth at their disposal, to produce. You would, without need of further argument with theorists, be convinced of the dramatic aptitude of the Shemitic race. Our art-critics deny them the dramatic capacity, for no other reason than that they spurn the crutch which we find essential for walking, that they have the power of producing, with no other means than the human organs, effects which our most elaborate machinery is unable to produce.

But this is not the place nor time for elaborate art discussion; of more importance to our present study is the evidence of their creative dramatic power as evinced in literature. This we will glance at a moment ere we take up once more the thread of our Psalms.

Going no further than Hebrew literature, I would call your attention to the Book of Job and the Song of Songs, as characteristically representative of the two types under which the drama is usually classed—tragedy and comedy.

Tragedy is that form of the drama in which the characters are represented in conflict, usually with the powers of nature or of fate. That in most instances they succumb to these influences is purely accidental, and is neither inherent in tragedy, nor essential to its working out.

Comedy is that form of the drama in which the characters are represented at rest, the artistic object being to produce pleasure; its art, which is confined to agreeable situations, is of a much narrower range and on a lower plane than that of tragedy. Pleasure, of course, is an intellectual motive, but if amusement as distinguished from pleasure become its aim, it degenerates into farce, and loses all claim to be considered as art.

I know not in what literature there is to be found a more perfect and artistic tragedy than the Book of Job. The personal art of the poet is consummate, his own personality completely retiring behind that of his characters, which develop themselves out of what seems to be the very necessity of their situation. There is no indication of the artist's own surrounding; the knowledge or manners of his time have left no trace on the setting or development of his plot. It is impossible for us to gather from his drama, from what age, or religion, or race the artist has sprung. He is unapproached by any one, either of the Greek or English dramatists, in that suppression of himself which is the first qualification of the dramatic artist.

Observe the perfect art with which the plot is laid and developed.

In an epic prologue, almost Euripidean in form, covering the first two chapters of our version, the artist accomplishes at the very outset, what Sophocles, in his prologues, so thoroughly understands how to do. He excites our interest in the occurrences to be brought forward, acquaints us with the hidden motive lying concealed from the actors, and dexterously ties the knot of the puzzle, which the subsequent action is to disentangle. I cannot, with justice to the subject, in the moment during which alone I can speak of this drama, make clear to you the masterly way in which the plot is developed. How the action rises with increasing δέσις, or mystery, during the first three scenes; how through the skilful interlude formed by the speech of Elihu (a lay figure), it passes to the λύσις or solution, first through its unravelment in the consciousness of the hero, leading him to an humble concession of his wrong, and lastly, by its disentanglement in outward reality, through the appearance of Jehovah as a Deus Vindex, reconciling the dualism which lies at the base of all tragedy, and whose solution the Greek dramatists groped after in vain. It is, from beginning to end, a stream of most dramatic action, as in Goethe's Tasso, the external action being compensated for by the life and precision with which the characters are drawn; their ideas are worked into incidents, which are brought, as it were, before the eye. If you follow the struggle depicted in the mind of the hero, while grappling with the problems to man the most insoluble, his alternations of faith and distrust, hope and black despair, and finally triumphant confidence, you will see that he is no less a tragic hero than the Œdipus of the Sophoclean drama. Even the minor art of the drama is perfect in kind, as in the painting of the three friends with whom the reader at first takes sides, gradually grows indifferent, and, at last, without any conscious break or compulsion from the artist, finds himself drawing away from them to the side of the hero.

Did we examine the more poetic side of this drama, and notice the inexhaustible wealth of thought, the keenness of psychological analysis, the deep knowledge of human motive, the wide acquaintance with the ever varying mood of nature, the power to paint human passion, and man, as acted on by the mysterious forces of nature, the originality and vigor of the poetic intuition, the richness of the fancy, the chaste beauty of the color which never shows a shade too much, we could justly join in the summing up of a recent commentator, that neither the Hindus, nor the Greeks, nor the English, have produced such a lofty and purely perfected drama. We may, most nearly, compare it with the tragedies of Æschylus or Shakspere, but we can find among these not a single one which approaches its depth of thought or perfection of form. It is the greatest tragedy of the world's literature. Does it not seem, therefore, incredible that the people who have produced the great master and masterpiece of the drama, should, by our latter day critics, be denied all capability for dramatic art?

Comedy we saw, as distinguished from tragedy whose basal idea is that of man's conflict and struggle with the forces which surround him, is the painting of still life, the development of character under those influences which are normal to it, our present idea of the humorous as connected with it being unessential and accidental. Bearing this definition in mind, you will not misunderstand me when I say, that the literary form of the Song of Songs is what, in the literature of other peoples, we should call comedy. But at the outset 1 decline to venture on any explanation of this book, as I have myself found, when studying it, no less than forty-seven different interpretations among Christian scholars alone, and how many more there may be I do not know.

The outcome of the varied and heated discussions of this book has been to show that it is a drama developing a complete action through the representation of character. The motive of the plot is the one, which, old as the world, is ever new. We know the hero was Solomon. The heroine is addressed in words as the Shulamite (vi., 13) and we have clear traces of a chorus of women referred to as the "Daughters of Jerusalem." This is the surely gained ground, but when we leave it we are at sea. Scholars of equal learning tell us that Solomon is the virtuous hero, or that he is playing a rôle similar to Faust's with Gretchen; that the Shulamite is the daughter of an Egyptian king, or that she is a simple country maiden beguiled to Jerusalem from her home in the vale of Shulem; that the chorus carries with the hero and heroine the whole action, or that there are at least twelve chief actors accompanied with a numerous troupe of shepherds and vintagers; that the finale is Solomon's marriage, or that it is the return of the

Shulamite to her rustic lover; that it is a pastoral drama which grew up at the harvest feasts in the kingdom of Ephraim; that it is a play written by Solomon for the summer theatre in his garden, or most marvelous of all, for which we are indebted to M. Renan, that it is a chance libretto of the royal opera company of Jerusalem; that it was written in the tenth century; that it was not written until the first century, and under the influence of the Greek erotic poets.

Oriental scholarship makes a ridiculous and melancholy spectacle of itself in the hopeless way with which it is ever anew attacking, and ever is baffled by this literary and linguistic riddle. As I said, I have no explanation of it to offer, for I make no pretence to understand it, and have not the slightest idea by whom or for what purpose it was written. So much may be agreed on, that in literary form it belongs to those compositions we call dramas, and that under this we must assign it to comedy. Whether written for public representation or not, it is impossible to say, though its composition for such a purpose, if proven, could have no effect on any sacred character we may assign to it.

As a help in studying this book, we may recall the Miracle-Plays which sprang up in the middle ages around the service of the church, written by the clergy for the teaching of religious truth, performed in the church at Eastertide, or some other feast day, and exercising, among a rude and unlettered community, an influence for good, far beyond that of the spoken word. I am inclined to believe that the literary origin of this mysterious book, may some time be found to have been for the religious instruction of the people gathered at one of the Temple feasts. For the present it is certainly very puzzling. A single word as to the art of the author, and I am through with the discussion of this book.

Art in comedy, we have seen, is, from its necessary limitations, inferior to that of tragedy, and so it would not be fair to compare the art of this book with that of Job. In my personal study, I have been wont to make use, as a means of comparison, of Hariri, an Arab poet of the eleventh century, who is the master of Shemitic comedy, in much the same way that Molière is of the Indo-European comedy. The comparison is to the disadvantage of the author of the Song of Songs. He is not destitute of pictorial power, but his art is crude and rudimental, the author seemingly lacking that grasp of human nature, which is almost as essential to the comedian as to the tragedist. If you wish a comparison from English literature, I would say he stands related to Hariri, somewhat as Chapman to Shakspere.

The question has further been raised whether there be not dramatic song in the Psalter. This we will endeavor to answer in our further study of it, to which we now return.

We had, in the last hour, finished the study of the Third Book, which brought us as far as Psalm xc., in our collection. We now proceed with the Fourth Book, which is one of the shorter collections which make up our Psalter, including the seventeen songs which are numbered in the English version xc.–cvi., inclusive.

The collector borrows two of these songs, ci., ciii., from the early Davidic Temple Book, to which we have had such frequent occasion to refer. Neither of them is poetically or historically of importance, and they need not long detain us.

Psalm ci. has for its author a king about entering on his reign, who compiles for the guidance of his conduct this poetical *vade mecum* of proverbial sayings and maxims. There is no reason of weight for doubting the personal Davidic authorship.

Psalm ciii. is one of the Psalms to which the canon of grammatical form spoken of in one of our early lectures can be applied. Its form is so Aramaic, more Aramaic in fact than any of the other Psalms in this book, that it is impossible to see how it could have arisen until some period when the Aramaic began to act on the Hebrew. It is consequently one of the latest songs in the Davidic Book. It was written for the religious song of the people as they were assembled at one of the feasts, probably Passover, and is one of the few songs in the Psalter which were primarily designed for congregational or popular use, as distinguished from the liturgic use of the Temple choirs. Of this kind of song it is the best specimen we have, and there are but few songs in the Psalter which exert, on the modern religious consciousness, so strong an impression as does this Psalm, written in half patois.

The large majority of the Songs in this Fourth Book, fourteen out of seventeen, are anonymous. In the last hour we saw that in the main the anonymous Psalms had a twofold source, either the ballad poetry of the people, or the liturgic ritual of the Temple, with a small remainder of songs whose personal origin is clear, being taken from verbal tradition, and remaining anonymous simply because the collectors were not able to ascertain the authorship. All these classes we at that time sufficiently illustrated.

A somewhat different sort of Psalm from any we have met with hitherto in our study is the first of these anonymous Psalms in the Fourth Book, Psalm xci., which is a dramatic song. The motive is didactic, to show the security from all harm of those who trust in Jehovah. This is developed dramatically by the poet through the use of two voices. When through their mutual speech and reply the thought has reached its height, a third voice, that of Jehovah, is introduced, confirming and ratifying the trust which has been placed in Him. In speaking of the drama a moment since, I said that there were supposed to be many dramatic songs in our Psalter, but the view as generally held seems to me to be a mistake. What are usually called dramatic songs are no more than antiphonal chants, or at the most, arrangements for various voices in the Temple choir. There are but one or two Psalms in which the poet's imagination has worked dramatically, that is, has developed itself through the action or voice of others. The present Psalm is one of the clearest examples of this method.

Psalm xcii., as the inscription informs us, was a "Song for the Sabbath Day," and we know was the one sung at the early sacrifice, at day-break, on Sabbath morning. As the stars began to appear on the previous evening, the Temple was closed, and the priests and Temple servants, who were to officiate on the morrow, were locked in a large room not far from the altar Here they rested as best they could on the stone benches, in their every-day attire, the only luxury allowed them being to make a bundle of their outer garments on which to rest their heads. About two o'clock they were waked by one of the rounds of the night guard, and after casting lots for their various duties, proceeded by torch-light to the onerous task of preparing the Temple and altar for the worship of the coming day. All was ready long before light, and with the first gloaming, a priest ascended the Eastern tower to watch for the coming of the sun. As its limb tipped the horizon, he gave a shout to those below, and the *tamid* (תָּמִיד), or morning sacrifice, was immediately commenced. Hastily bringing a lamb from the Temple stalls (a description of which would not increase our admiration of the worship), it was slaughtered and laid on the altar, ere it had become full day. As the offering began the Temple choir struck up this Psalm. While they were singing it, the great doors of the Temple were thrown back, and the multitude came thronging in to early worship. Somewhat later in the morning, for the benefit of the upper and wealthy classes, as well as those whose devotion was not of a nature to lead them to bestir themselves at daybreak, there was a minor sacrifice, called *musaph* (מוּסָף), the time of which was regulated by convenience or the season of the year. At this a part of the song from Deuteronomy xxxii. was sung. In the afternoon again, not far from three or four o'clock, there was what we might call an even-song service. The offering named *minha* (מִנְחָה), was a simple one of cakes of fine flour covered with oil, and was accompanied by the singing of several selections from the songs of Exodus xv., and Numbers xxi. It was finished as twilight was coming on, and with it, ended the Temple services of the Sabbath.

Psalm xciii. seems a fragment of an older song. Its words and melody are winged with great freshness of expression. It was the regular Friday Psalm in the Temple.

Psalm xciv. is a late Psalm. The author shows the effect of the Davidic method in which he had been trained, yet is not without a little vein of pungent irony peculiar to himself.

Psalm xcv. was written for a Temple song, and was used in its liturgy in a way not dissimilar to its present use in the Anglican church. It is held in general terms, and contains no indication either of authorship or situation.

Psalm xcvi. is of similar origin with Psalm xcv. We can determine its time of composition, as in the Second Temple, from the thought running through it that Judaism is for the whole world, and not alone for a single people. This higher idea of the universal mission of their religion did not become part of the common thought of Israel, until the destruction of their Temple, and exile among the stranger, had broken down the barriers of their old intolerance.

The author of Psalm xcvii. must have been a diligent reader of Isaiah, whose thought and language he ever reflects and borrows.

Psalms xcviii., xcix. are Temple songs, which demand no special mention.

Psalm c. is of the same kind, but worthy of attention for its clear and elegant style.

Psalm cii. has the remarkable inscription that it was written by an unfortunate man who was in exile. It is his prayer for the restoration of himself and his people to their land, and for the rebuilding of Jerusalem which lay in ruins. There can be, therefore, no doubt as to the time of its composition. In a few places the author shows great poetic power, but as an offset he lacks consecutive thought, and lucid arrangement. Who he was we know as little as did the Psalm collector.

Psalms cv., cvi. are long compilations of reminiscences from the early history of the people, arranged for the antiphonal chanting of the Temple choirs. Even in the English translation they show clearly their art and their origin. They are fair instances of the epical method, and confirm what we said of it in our previous lecture.

In Psalm civ., the last of these anonymous Psalms,

we find one of the most noteworthy songs in our Psalter, although poetically it is not to be compared with many other of these songs, and its grammatical forms show traces of a speech which was rapidly passing into desuetude. In this connection I wish to call your attention to the fact, that the two Psalms which are intellectually the strongest, this and the one hundred and thirty-ninth, are both anonymous, and both in a style showing traces of Aramaic influence. It is one of the factors which were used in making up the famous theory of a Ten Tribe Song Book, as it was called, whence these and many other of the Psalms were supposed to be taken.

The singer is a man of disciplined rather than cultured mind, one who has received the most advanced scientific training of his day. He looks abroad on nature and gathers together its diverse phenomena into the most perfect cosmos which antiquity has produced. It is with a scholar's eye he searches it through; he arranges his matter under accurate and orderly classifications. His very nomenclature shows a trained, it was on the tip of my pen to write, biologist, when I bethought myself of the authority on which we are told that biology is a science not yet fifty years old. The scholar's conclusion is that the whole course of visible life he has studied is but the effect of an unseen inscrutable power. In this power he discerns such traces of order, of thought, and of adaptation as to lead him to affirm personality; such further traces of care and guidance that he breaks forth into the exclamation, "How manifold are thy works! in wisdom hast thou made them all." The author is a man of Aristotelian mind. He belongs to the straitest sect of the Realists; his observation of phenomena is as keen as, if not keener than, that of any of the Empiricists; his knowledge of nature is wider than that of the Greek Peripatetics; his conception of it reaches a height to which even Platonists did not soar. It is the mood of the present to speak of Aristotle as the father of natural science, and yet here is a scholar of an alien race and two centuries earlier, who has been observing, collecting, and sifting the phenomena of nature and the organic life which surround him, and deducing from them a principle of orderly arrangement, and of motion through some hidden power. There are some other sciences beside theology whose histories need rewriting.

It is in a Psalm like this, written by a careful and inquiring scholar who shows no trace of the superstition of the vulgar, that we may best gain an idea of the crude scientific knowledge of that early time, and of the Hebrew people, which has been a stumbling-block to so many. The writers of Scripture believe and tell us in their writings that the earth was a plane surface, square in form, supported at each corner by pillars resting on the rocky bed of the sea which surrounded it; that its geographical centre was Judea and Jerusalem; that underneath it was an enormous cavern called Sheol, through which flitted the shades of the departed; that the vault above was a cube of metal, placed like a tent-cover over the earth, and fastened down at its corners; that to this cover all the heavenly bodies were attached, and on it they moved round for the gratification or benefit of the earth, which was the centre and reason of the whole creation; that in this overhanging arch there were windows, through which, when opened, there descended the rain or snow from their storehouses just above. But enough—their science, as we said in the last hour of their ethics, was precisely that of their contemporary and contiguous peoples. It was not their mission to teach science to the world, and their inspiration has not eliminated their ignorance of it. Their mission was a religious one; their eyes were opened to behold the hidden meaning in the phenomena they so imperfectly comprehended. Our singer teaches that the world sprang from a divine idea, grew up through the development of a carefully matured plan, and is guided by a perfect order which is the expression of the divine will. Compare him with the contemporary, or at least not long subsequent physicists of the Ionian school: Thales who taught that a chaotic water was the origin of all—Anaximenes who saw the beginning of life in a subtle and potent ether—Heraclitus who believed that a fire self-kindled and self-extinguishable had set in motion the sequence of phenomena we call life and nature—or even with Anaxagoras, who, rising higher, saw the influence of a mind in the arrangement of matter, and you will perceive what in our Psalm is local color and the ignorance common to the writer's age, and what the truth for all time of which he had caught an intuition.

Each of the three books, which we have hitherto studied, had some distinctive peculiarity. That of the First Book was its exclusive use of older Davidic material—that of the Second Book the Songs of Korah—that of the Third Book the Asaphian poems. In this Fourth Book it is the Psalm, attributed by its inscription to Moses, the only Psalm in the entire Psalter referred by the editors to a period prior to David. The fable of the later Jewish schoolmen, that certain of the Psalms were written by one or another of the Patriarchs, does not command credence enough to warrant our considering it. The various views as to the accuracy of the editor's inscription have naturally been measured by the commentator's opinion as to Moses and the Mosaic age. On external grounds it has been questioned for some marvellous reasons; either because there was no such man as Moses, it being but a mythical name around which had clustered the tradition of the foretime, or granting his existence, he was either on the one hand a rude desert Sheik, untrained to an elaborate art such as this song displays, or he was just the reverse, a court servant of the Pharaohs, moved by some personal indignity to incite a revolt among his people; a weakling who shrank, through sheer incapacity, from the first shock of battle with the hill tribes on the northern edge of the desert; that he was murdered secretly during a mutiny of the people, and his expedition saved by Joshua, with the aid of an allied Bedouin chief, named Caleb. Such being the assumed fact, he was of course incapable of composing a song of such ethical purity and sublime religious faith.

These theories as to Moses are not hid in a corner, but elaborated with scholarship and skill in histories of the Orient which are accessible to you all. I believe myself they are capable of such convincing historical disproof as to have no weight in our judgment as to the authorship of this Psalm, but bear in mind, that our judgments on this, and all points similar to it which are constantly rising in our study of Hebrew literature, are only of value when determined on historical ground. No scholar can afford to pooh-pooh, as inherently ridiculous, any theory which represents the careful work and conscientious thought of any human mind capable of investigating the literary or scientific phenomena at issue. Any science, which allows any consideration save the attainment of truth to be a factor in its study, is sure to be the worst loser. Hebrew literature has suffered well-nigh irrecoverably from the merciless way with which even in the circle of scholars, whose only aim in life should be the discovery of truth, the odium of personal ostracism has been visited upon all who have arrived at views in regard to it running counter to their age.

Neither Moses, nor any other character of history, suffers from the most searching historical examination. Just as was said in a former hour when we were speaking of David, we may now say in respect to the historical character of Moses, that it has been as satisfactorily established as that of Charlemagne, or William of Normandy, or in fact as the existence of any one whom we have not ourselves seen.

The more common denial of the Mosaic authorship of the Psalm has been from internal grounds of allusion and style. The singer is an aged man, who, almost alone in his generation, has reached the threescore and ten years which seem the limit of life. In this exquisite meditation he looks back over his generation, comparing the vanity and shortness of human life with the everlasting existence and power of God. His poem is an artistic one. Some of the touches, as the figure of man and the grass of the field, are as daintily worked as those in the Korahite Book. His thought is elevated, his intuition of the meaning of life deep, his religious spirit refined; whoever he may be, he must have been a man of genius. I do not grasp the force of the historical allusions which have led many scholars to refer its composition to the later monarchy. The allusions of the song are held in general terms, bearing no stamp of any particular age; none of them are unsuited to what we know of the Mosaic times. When we come to closely scrutinize the language of the Psalm, we find startling resemblances to the two poems known as the Song and Blessing of Moses in Deuteronomy xxxii., xxxiii., all of them showing traces of the same hand and artistic method. The question of the authorship of Psalm xc. depends in the last resort, as do so many other literary questions, on our judgment as to the authorship of the Pentateuch. Do we decide that Moses wrote the songs in Deuteronomy, the argument of style will irresistibly lead us to believe he wrote this Psalm.

As to its transmission to the collector of our Book, there can be no difficulty. Speaking of it in another connection we showed that the Psalm was not taken from the older Davidic Temple Book, else it would have been cited; nor was it transmitted through the mouth of the people, which would have blurred its dainty lines, but it could well have been preserved in the early song book, "The Book of Valor," whence the writers of Joshua and Samuel have drawn so freely. We do not know that it did come from there, but the possibility of it removes the difficulty.

We come now to consider when, and by whom, this Fourth Book of the Psalter, whose songs we have been examining in detail, was collected. That you may clearly judge of it, we must first briefly sketch for you the history of the period immediately succeeding Nehemiah, who was the collector of the Second and Third Books.

Of Nehemiah's history subsequent to the thirty-second year of Artaxerxes, to which we traced it in the last hour, we know nothing. It seems probable that he remained at his post as Persian commissioner until the year 405 B. C., when he would have been between sixty and seventy years old, and then returned to Persia and died there. His character as a man of culture and of letters, and as an administrator of sagacity and decision, we have already sketched. The period of seventy-two years, between his death and the battle of Issus, is almost a blank in Jewish history. The people had been won for the Persian cause by the policy of Nehemiah, and to it they remained loyal, even in the face of the advancing armies of Alexander.

There seems, indeed, at one time, to have been a movement toward a league with Egypt, but it was, doubtless, no more than an intrigue of the aristocracy, whose traditional policy inclined them toward an Egyptian alliance, somewhat as the policy of the Scotch nobles always favored alliance with France. The people were under the immediate control of the High Priest, who was, in turn, responsible to the Persian Satrap of Syria, for the payment of the imposts and the preservation of order. The names of the High Priests during this period, until the time of Alexander, are preserved in the Chronicles, forming one of the norms for determining the age of that book. They belonged to a family famous alone for its vices, and equally notorious for its corruption with the family of Caiaphas, who held the sacerdotal office at the beginning of our era. The High Priestship became an object of intrigue, was bought and sold in the palace of the Persian Satrap who held the right of preferment, and saw in the price of investiture one of his richest emoluments.

Almost the only information preserved to us from this period, is of a fratricidal quarrel in the Temple, between the High Priest Jochanan and his brother Jesus, who had been intriguing against him with the Satrap. The High Priest assassinates his brother in the Holy Place, the fighting priests have to be driven asunder by a body of Persian soldiery, and a seven years' penance is laid on the city. But do not let us call it a dark age, until we recall how one Easter day, scarce ten years ago, in the same city, Greek and Latin monks brained one another with their crosiers in the very sepulchre of our Lord, until expelled at the point of Turkish bayonets. The world does move, but history just as truly repeats itself.

Historians tell us that it was a time of quiet internal development among the people, but even that we do not know. During the wars and disorders throughout hither Asia, which foretold the dissolution of the Persian power, and prepared an easy victory for Alexander, who should be called the Lucky rather than the Great, Palestine could not have escaped unscathed, and must have been more or less harried by the Greek mercenaries who marched hither and thither across it, in the pay of Artaxerxes Ochus, against the Phenician and Egyptian towns. They were fortunately too weak to assume a prominent rôle in the troubled politics of the times, and the events of it were not momentous enough to leave any record of themselves either in their traditions or literature.

The cloud no bigger than a man's hand, which had been gathering over the Persian empire under Philip of Macedon, burst into a storm under his son Alexander. In the battle of Issus near Tarsus, fought 333, B. C., seventy-two years after Nehemiah left the stage, Darius was defeated, largely through his own bad manœuvering, and the Persian power was irretrievably broken. Judging it imprudent to leave in his rear an enemy so formidable as the Phenician commercial towns whose fleets were threatening the coasts of Greece, Alexander immediately pushes into Palestine, and lays siege to Tyre, which is not captured until after a stubborn siege of seven months. Gaza also makes a show of resistance which is speedily crushed, and toward the close of the year 332 Alexander advances against Jerusalem, which saves itself from pillage by a timely submission and opening of its gates. The story of his reception by a white-robed procession, his obeisance to the High Priest, and his sacrifice in the Temple, contains too many anachronisms to be possible. It is a legend coming from the Alexandrian Jews, by whom it was fabricated to bring their nation and religion into honorable connection with the Greek conqueror of the Orient.

With the capture of Jerusalem, a new era begins for the Jewish people; intellectually, through their contact with the occidental mind and the Greek literature; commercially, through their enforced settlement in Alexandria, and their dispersion as traders throughout the then civilized world. We cannot, however, follow it. In the seventy-three years we have just been reviewing, the Fourth Book of our Psalter had its origin, and we are only concerned with the history of the time, as throwing light on this. It was not a period of intellectual activity among the Jews; there may have been some minor writers, but their productive age was past; the scholars and literary men of this period were, for the most, collectors and editors of the earlier literature.

In what contrast stand these seventy-three years in the literature of their conquerors!

This three-quarters of a century was the hey-day of the splendid literary development of the Greeks. Three years before its opening the father of history had died in Italy; two years later died Euripides, the dramatist of human passion, followed in the year with which the period opens, by Sophocles, the dramatist of character. In its early years, Thucydides, whose unrivalled descriptive power and brevity of style make him the master of Greek prose, had met his violent death, and Socrates had taught morals and drank the hemlock in Athens. Toward the middle of the period Plato was teaching in the Academy, Xenophon campaigning through Asia Minor, and Aristotle was walking in the porticoes of the Lyceum. These are merely the greatest names. In some part of the same period lived Agathon, Philemon and Menander; Zeno, Epicurus and Pyrrho; Lysias, Isäus and Demosthenes. It is a galaxy of names within a single century to which no other people can offer a parallel.

That the Greeks at this time knew anything of the Jews is improbable; that their scholars knew the Jewish literature is quite impossible. The stories of Plato's acquaintance with the Hebrew Scripture, and of the intercourse of Aristotle with Hebrew scholars are fictions of the Greek Fathers, who were unable to recognize any truth outside of revelation. Yet there was being silently collected among this obscure and feeble people a literature which was destined, not only to rival the Greek, but greatly to surpass it in its influence on the thought and culture of all coming time. If the Greeks knew them it was only as a barbarous upland folk, but they had already developed a poetry more delicate and refined in form, with deeper intuition of nature, than any thing which the culture and genius of the Greeks ever produced.

Who collected the Fourth Book of our Psalter, and to what time within this period its collection is to be referred, we cannot, from lack of sufficient data, determine with any approach to accuracy.

278 *ORIGIN AND GROWTH OF THE PSALMS.*

From the number of purely liturgical songs we might be led to suppose that the editor was some attaché of the Temple, either priest or Levite. And this would further be confirmed by what we know of the literary activity of the time, which centered around the Temple and its schools.

If in lieu of external testimony, or tradition, we make use of the internal literary evidence, and then carefully compare this book with the one immediately following, we shall probably reach this result, namely, that the Fourth Book was collected by some scholar in connection with the Temple, about the middle of the period between Nehemiah and the Greek conquest of Palestine, say not far from 370 B. C.

I say collected by some scholar, for if the literary evidence as to the collector's method which has shown us that the First Book was gathered by a priest, the Second and Third by a man of literary instinct and culture, be of any value here, it shows us that this Fourth Book was collected by some one who had the prepossessions of a scholar, and who wrought after a scholar's fashion.

In the next lecture we will consider the Fifth Book, and the final revision of all five books into the form in which they have come down to us as our Psalter.

The poetic cyclus of no other people, whether of ancient or modern times, can for a moment be put in comparison with that of the Shemites. Those of India and of Greece, which more commonly have been compared with it, are perceptibly inferior. The literature of India needs but to be read to see at what a remove, both in thought and expression it stands from the literature of the Shemites. I do not imagine that even its most devoted students would enter a claim for its stylistic superiority. Its value lies at other points which do not concern us here.

No one conversant with the literature both of the Shemites and the Hellens could venture to claim for the Shemitic mind the breadth, the subtlety, and the grasp of the Greek. The Greek intellect was more many-sided, if I be pardoned the vulgarism, than that of any people who have left a literature. It touched in some way all the keys which the Shemite did, beside very many which were beyond his reach.

For many things, as philosophy and plastic art in which the Greeks have remained masters of the world, the Shemitic mind had no adaptation. Their art meant either the huge or the grotesque—were Solomon's Temple restored we should think it barbarous. Their psychological analysis was deep and acute, their observation of phenomena accurate and extensive, but philosophy and science were alike impossible to minds incapable of constructing a synthesis. It was perhaps for this very reason that the few keys they do touch resound with greater sweetness and volume. I imagine that no one widely read in both Greek and Shemitic poetry would have any hesitation to which to award the palm. I would not go as far in my statement as one of the greatest German poets of our century, Friedrich Rückert, who said that when wearied with Homer he would refresh himself with a draught of the desert air which effervesces like champagne through the Songs of the Hamasa. Individual comparisons, whether between books or persons, are always odious and unjust, though the Psalms or Hamasa need not flinch even this issue.

The only fair comparison is gained by the study of an entire literature, and what I mean to say is, that tried by the canons of pure art, the Shemitic poetic literature is unexcelled by any other.

I hope to have space for the comparison between Greek and Shemitic poetry in the next hour; if, however, it be then of necessity crowded out, as it has been from this hour, I shall crave your permission to call your attention to it at some future time.

LECTURE IX.

I HARDLY know whether the more to congratulate my audience or myself on nearing the end of our journey through the Psalm country. I fear the road may have been wearisome to you, but am not without hope that we may have obtained by the way some outlooks into Shemitic poetry, and the habit of the Shemitic mind, which will prove repaying.

We have so much to compass, or rather to strive to compass, in the brief space of this final hour, that, without further prelude, we must proceed with our study from where we were obliged to leave off at the close of the last lecture.

We have considered, in order and at length, four books of our Psalter; there now alone remains the fifth and last book.

The Fifth Book is the longest of the Psalter collections, containing the forty-four songs, which, in our

English version, are numbered Psalms cvii.–cl. We find, on examination, as might be gleaned from its position, that it is the latest of these books, and, though containing some few remarkable poems, it leaves upon the reader the impression of marked inferiority to the other collections. However, we must deal justly with it, by hastily summarizing for you its contents

The collector has made a large draft on the early "Davidic Temple Book," with which you are all ere now, from frequent mention, well acquainted. He borrows from it no less than fifteen songs, more than one-third of his collection, differing thus noticeably from the collectors of the two previous books, who, between them, borrow from the Davidic Book only three songs.

The first of these, Psalm cviii., is of great interest as showing us the method of the collector's workmanship. When discussing that question in an early lecture, we dwelt sufficiently on this Psalm. We saw that it was a purely liturgic cento, made up of fragments from two older songs, Psalms lvii. and lx. We also endeavored to show that the liturgic arranger had before him our Second Psalter Book, from whence, and not from the older Davidic Book, the selections of which the Psalm is composed have been taken. Consequently, the Psalm can only merit its inscription as Davidic, in the sense that the diverse material of which it is made up, all came originally from the Davidic collection.

Psalm cix. is one of the Psalms spoken of in our seventh lecture, as showing traces of a vindictive expression foreign to our present standards both of ethics and religion. None of us could join with the singer in wishing, even against our bitterest enemy, that his children might become vagabonds, and his widow an outcast. It is but the local color reflecting a rude age, and a barbarous civilization, which we do not regard imitable, which we ought not to consider commendable.

Psalm cx. has, from its peculiarly prophetic character, been the subject of as much discussion as any other song in our Psalter. It brings into more prominence, than any passage even in the prophetic literature, the Messianic idea running through the Old Testament, which has formed its chief claim religiously on the Christian Church. This, however, is a secondary meaning, not inhering in the literary form, and one which, in this study, designed to be purely literary and objective, I have studiously striven to avoid. Hebrew literature is one of the most cultured and refined in the world; the prevailing judgment among literary men as to its obscurity and inelegance, is the prejudgment either of ignorance or indolence. It yields to the Greek alone in breadth and grasp; it surpasses it in beauty of color, depth of feeling and intensity of expression. No other literature, save the Greek, is comparable to it. It has therefore been my aim, as I well know but imperfectly attained, to interest you in the neglected literary study of the Psalter, rather than to dwell on interpretations and expositions accessible to you in the current books of the time. Hence we pass this Psalm with the single remark, that though of the utmost historical importance, and the keystone of the Messianic interpretations of the Old Testament, it is rather disjointed and rugged poetry. I read it one evening after I had been looking through Robert Browning's "Inn Album" which had then lately appeared, and it struck me it must have had somewhat the same effect on the mind of the poet's contemporaries, that the " Inn Album " had just had on mine.

Psalm cxxxviii. is quite lame enough in metre to have been written by Jeremiah to whom it is referred by the Septuagint. We have had occasion before to refer to Jeremiah's unfortunate and eccentric style, but there is really no reason to hold him guilty of all the halting verse in the Psalter. There is nothing in it to detain us from passing on to Psalm cxxxix., which is intellectually the strongest poem not only in this collection, but in the entire Psalter.

Psalm cxxxix. may justly be placed side by side with Psalm civ., which we considered in the last hour. It is not, however, by the same author, for though the Aramaism of the language points to its production in the same period, the style and touch are essentially dissimilar. The author of Psalm civ. was a student of nature and of physical science; the author of Psalm cxxxix. is a psychologist, or student of the human mind. His method is that of the school known in the present parlance as phenomenalist. Even through the poetic clothing of the thought, his mind works, from the physical basis of life up through its phenomenal expression in conscious action, in a way startlingly similar to that of a lately deceased English historian of philosophy, who, I fear, did not include the name of this, his earliest forerunner, in his sketch of the development of the world's thought.[1] He differs from the modern phenomenalist alone in his result, which is, that the external phenomena indicate that all life is a single entity, which he regards as one of the manifestations of Deity. On this result he further builds up a theory, that the human soul is kindled by the bestowal of a part of this entity on the organism already developed and prepared for it; through

[1] G. H. Lewes. (T.)

the outworking of this applied force in the physical phenomena of life, the data are to be collected which lead to a sure definition of its nature. But this is technical. The singer is a man of introspective mind, who has been investigating and subtly analyzing the phenomena of his personality and conscious life. With a rigorous induction and rarely lucid statement, he traces these back to their fountain-head, the soul; this soul he teaches is an emanation of the Deity. How much of his philosophy is the reflection of the thought of his time, or of the mystic theosophy which has been the peculiar habit of the Oriental mind from the earliest times, we can not now inquire, nor even give space for a comparison of him with Pythagoras and contemporaneous thinkers in Greece.

He represents the highest achievements of the Hebrew, I had almost said Shemitic, mind, in the domain of mental science, for the Shemitic racial habit does not predispose it to excellence in this field. With their acute and painfully minute analysis, there seems, for the most part, utterly lacking that synthesis, or grouping of things according to their analogies, through which the facts are led back to causes, the phenomena arranged under principles, and thus a philosophic conception gained of the operations and laws, either of mind or of matter. The Shemitic mind is, more than the Indo-European, endowed with those faculties which give birth to speculative research—curiosity, imagination, reflection and analysis. There are, besides, few families of language so rich in terms appropriate to philosophical inquiry, so indicative of analytical research among the people who coined them, as the Shemitic.

The psychological nomenclature of the Hebrew is well-nigh as highly and delicately articulated as that of the Greek. Why they lacked the further historical, logical, and synthetic faculty with which the Greeks were so richly endowed, we do not see any necessary reason, either in their mental habit, or environment. Anthropology has no adequate solution to offer, and probably never will have. Racial peculiarities are of a kind with personal characteristics, and an explanation of their genesis is baffled by problems equally recondite.

It is for this reason that the history of philosophy has been the history of the development of the Aryan mind. What answers to philosophy in native Shemitic literature is acute proverbial sayings, or minute observations of the phenomena of mind or matter, which the thinker lacked power to grasp into a generalization. The Talmud contains more original and epigrammatic observations of phenomena than any book in Hebrew literature, yet remains a hopelessly irredeemable mass of *disjecta membra*. It furnished the brick and mortar; the Hebrew mind lacked power to build. It is true there grew up in Alexandria a semi-Shemitic school of philosophy, the new Platonism, but it was the product of the Shemitic mind fructified by Greek thought.

Arab philosophy is a myth—the Arab mind is incapable of philosophy. The so-called Arab philosophers were foreigners who had learned the Aristotelian philosophy, and reproduced it in a manner more or less accurate, with almost no originality, in the Arabic, which since the seventh century has been the French of the East. Avicenna was a Turk, Averroes a Moor, Maimonides a Jew. With equal reason the French might claim Leibnitz as one of their philosophers.

The remaining six Psalms, cxl.–cxlv., attributed by their inscription to the Davidic collection, are neither historically or poetically of importance enough to detain us, and offer no peculiarities in form or style, which we have not considered in speaking of the other books.

Psalm cxli. is of interest from its having been the vesper song of the early Church.

Psalm cxlii. has an editorial note, that it was written in the cave, but whether of Adullam or En gedi we have no further information.

The Fifth Book also contains sixteen anonymous

Psalms. Of these, four are what are called alphabetic songs. Most noteworthy among them, and at the same time the longest in the Psalter, is the one numbered in our English version Psalm cxix. The art in an alphabetic poem is bric-a-brac, the same learned trifling that is exhibited in an acrostic. It is not the product of a creative or original mind or age, it is only possible when artificiality has replaced art—expression, thought—form, originality. This Psalm is, in its endless reiterations of the same idea through one hundred and seventy-six verses, monotonous, inartistic, common-place, the sole handicraft—not art, for it can lay no claim to that—displayed, is in so arranging the matter, that every eighth verse begins with a new letter of the alphabet; there is no trace of a developing and consecutive thought; no order or connection in the maxims which are loosely strung together. From one or two touches in the Psalm itself, it seems that the author was, both in captivity and imprisonment, so it has been concluded by the majority of scholars, that it was written by him to relieve the tedium of his confinement, a sort of effort to construct as many verses as possible on the same subject, and then arrange them under the letters of the alphabet with which they began. Solitary confinement is a situation which reduces even a strong mind to inanity. Out of sheer desperation men watch spiders, count straws, and possibly sometimes compose alphabetical poems. Who the imprisoned author was we do not know; it is a mere guess which assigns the poem to the High Priest Jonathan. The reason for its preservation in the Psalter, was probably the use of it for the instruction of the youths in the Temple schools, its alphabetic form adapting it to memorizing, which prevails far more in the Orient than among ourselves. We may explain it as somewhat of the same order of poetry as the celebrated rhyme beginning "In Adam's fall we sinned all," or any of the numberless productions in which the muse has been harnessed to teaching children the cardinal virtues, or the order of the books in the Scripture.

Of the three other alphabetic poems, Psalms cxi., and cxii. begin each verse with a new letter of the alphabet; in Psalm cxlv. it is every other verse. They seem to have been liturgic forms prepared for the worship of the common people, to whom the sequence of the letters would act as a suggestion and aid to the memory. In the later Judaism they came to be used as charms, the letters of the alphabet serving as a string of beads. The Talmud tells us, that whoever repeats Psalm cxlv., thrice a day, is sure of eternal life.

Of the anonymous Psalms in this collection, other

than the alphabetic, few are deserving of special note. Almost all of them are songs prepared for the Temple, fashioned after older models, devoid of original thought, barren of beauty of expression.

Psalms cxiii.–cxviii. form what is called the Hallel (הַלֵּל הַמִּצְרִי, Egyptian Hallel or Song of Praise) sung by the people on their various feasts. In the social service on Passover evening there was sung, when drinking the fourth glass of wine at the end of the meal, Psalm cxv.–cxviii., which is doubtless the hymn sung by Christ and his followers at the close of the Last Supper.

Psalm cxv., the "non nobis Domine," when used in the Temple service was sung by the officiating priest over the offering which he was presenting to Jehovah.

Psalm cxvii., the shortest Psalm, is really the two closing verses of Psalm cxvi., which only a misadventure to one of the early manuscripts has converted into a separate Psalm.

We must pass by Psalm cxviii., the processional with which the restored Temple was reëntered, and Psalms cxxxv., cxxxvi., which are arranged for the antiphonal chanting of the Temple choirs.

Psalm cxxxvii. is an exquisite bit of lyric song written in Babylon, on whose willows the unknown singer had hung his harp. The softness of its elegiac measure makes it artistically one of the most attractive of the Psalms.

Psalms cxlvi., cxlvii., are doxological Psalms with which the service was closed, being placed very appropriately at the end of the collection. Several of them have interesting historical situations to which we cannot allude.

Psalm cxlviii. should be noticed for the broad touch and strong relief with which the artist paints the picture of the whole creation joining in the praises of Jehovah. As I stood once in the Sistine Chapel, studying, in its half twilight, the mural paintings which have made their artist immortal, it flashed across my mind that this Psalm, which I had heard not long before in the service, was in poetry, just what the "Last Judgment" was in painting.

Psalm cxlix. has very often in history kindled rebellions, fanned the fires of martyrdom, or led the forces of persecution. It was the favorite hymn to which inquisitors kindled their auto-da-fé. In the Thirty Years' War, it was the battle cry with which Tilly's forces, the representatives of barbarism and reaction, charged on the Swedes, and has been the watch-word of innumerable peasant revolts both in England and on the Continent.

There yet remains for us to consider the most important part poetically of the Fifth Book, the collection of fifteen short songs, numbered in our version cxx.-cxxxiv., bearing the inscription "Songs of Degrees." As to the meaning of the inscription you will find in the books a disagreement well nigh irreconcilable. The Talmud, as usual when there is doubt, chooses the most incredible and far-fetched explanation—here a silly story destitute alike of point or possibility. The early versions are hopelessly at sea; they partly transliterate and partly paraphrase. The later Jewish scholars call them "Songs of Steps," and invent a legend of their being sung from certain Temple steps on the eve of the feast days—it is probable there were no such steps in the Temple. Lastly most Christian scholars refer the name either to the metrical form, as a species of triolet, or to their musical accompaniment, as similar to a fugue, both foreign to what we know of Shemitic poetry and Shemitic music, while for neither theory is there the slightest evidence in the usage of the word, or the form of the songs themselves. All these interpretations are in common the result of the narrow literary culture, and exclusively theologic aim with which the Psalm poetry has been studied, and confirm the old adage that he who knows but one literature, knows no literature. Their freshness, their brilliant color, their allusions, their reflection of the homely phrase and surrounding of the folk, show them to have no other author than the mouth of the people. They were ballads which grew up around journeys, which, thrice in the year, were made from all the country round to the feasts in Jerusalem.

At Passover, at Harvest and at Tabernacles, the people flocked together from their farms and pastures, into their towns and villages, and in company of their neighbors and acquaintance, marched with music and with song to the shrine or Temple of Jehovah. It is a mistake to suppose that these feasts were purely religious. That was, no doubt, one element, but we further know that they served as great fairs, where the people bartered with one another, and whither the Phenician traders came to purchase; also there were games and trials of skill. In a word, they were not unlike the Greek games, whose origin was also religious. Just as in Olympia, Athenian and Spartan met together, forgetting all save that they were Hellens, so here, Danites from the slopes of Hermon, Simeonites from the desert of the South, Reubenites from the steppes of Moab, met together in Shiloh or Jerusalem, forgetting all save that they were Israelites; so not the least effect of these festivals was to cultivate the national patriotism, and create a bond of union for the national life.

During the feasts Jerusalem became the centre of commerce for all the surrounding countries, and in a rude age, when there was no circulation of literature, this concourse of the people, from all Israel, afforded the fittest audience for the recital of literary productions, and the publication of knowledge. How extensive the literature which grew up around these feasts we have no longer any means of ascertaining; doubtless, much as the Greek games, they afforded the motive for many works which have been lost to us. Around such gatherings, there always grows up a luxuriant ballad poetry, and our collector has gathered from it some of the choicest of those which were connected with their religious observance. The meaning of the inscriptions is, Songs of Upgoings, *i. e.*, Songs of Feast Journeys, or as sometimes paraphrased, "Pilgrim Songs."

Psalms cxxi., cxxii. seem to be the songs with which those who remain behind dismiss the pilgrims setting out for the feast, wishing Jehovah's blessing for their journey and return.

Psalm cxxiii. is the reply of the pilgrims.

Psalm cxxiv. is a vesper song of the company as they encamped for the night.

Psalm cxxv. the song when from the hills lying round about Jerusalem, they catch the first glimpse of the Holy City, and so on through all the songs, which are plainly referable to one or another situation during these festal journeys, or at the feasts themselves.

I wish I had time to analyze for you all these most perfect of the religious ballads of the Hebrew people, and then to supplement what Professor Child said to you last year of European ballads, by describing the ballad poetry of the Shemites. The choicest of them are Hebrew, but all the Hebrew ballads which are preserved to us being religious, they do not reflect the characteristic life and thought of the people as clearly as do the ballads of the Bedouin. At a future time I may present to you some studies in the ballad poetry of the Arabs. I am sure you would enjoy learning of the Moallakât, which, not unlike the "Songs of Degrees" in our Psalter, grew up around the pilgrimages to the ancient shrine at Mecca, the earliest Arab literature which has come down to us, a poetry wild, vast and monotonous as the desert whence it was born—of the Kasidâs, or Minnesongs, in which the lover, with a knightly courtesy more exquisite than any troubadour, sings his absent lady, the traveller his camel which bears him over gleaming and yellow sand, the warrior his sword and the joy of battle, the robber his swift horse and the nightly foray, the moralist the fleeting nature of life, which comes and goes like a tent in the desert, while eternal and changeless over all gleams, deep and mysterious, the blue heaven whose secret he could not read. Then when these roving shepherds had become the kings of the world, and dwelt in marble palaces amidst the orange groves of Cordova and Bagdad, there arose another minstrelsy which sang of nightly boatings by torch-light, of moonlight and the stars, of meetings in rose gardens, of palaces and villas, of mosques and cities, of statues and painting, of culture and luxury, and of the rough desert life from which their fathers had come. The world knows no more delicate poetry.

This Fifth Book, we can only say in finishing our cursory glance through it, does not show marks of a single and uniform effort in its collection, but seems rather to have been the work of several hands, with the aim of completing and supplementing the previous four collections.

It alone remains for us to ascertain, if possible, by whom and when all five books were collected together and edited in the form we now have them in our Psalter.

As to when, we would reply, that literary and historical reasons, which we endeavored to make clear to you in an early lecture, indicate that it must have been cast into its present form ere the Greek conquest of Palestine, B. C. 332, and that the possibility of one or two Psalms at a later day coming into the collection from the margin does not militate against this view, or weaken the strength of the argument.

Internal literary reasons lead us to believe that the same hands which collected the last book were those which edited the entire Psalter into the definitely final and authoritative shape which it ever after retained. As to who they were, we have neither information nor clear tradition. That it was not the work of a single individual, we saw a moment since when speaking of the Fifth Book. Most probably it was the work of the body of ecclesiastics and scholars in connection with the Temple, who collected and gave authority to almost all the writings in the Hebrew Scriptures. They seem to have made use of the four older collections, without essential change of text, or editorial revision, this being indicated by the repetition of the same song in different books, and by other proofs which you will recall our having alluded to from time to time. Their design was not to prepare a new book from older material, but to collect together the older books and issue them, with what seemed a necessary supplement, in a final and authoritative form.

I trust that the sequence of our story of the Psalm collection has been clear to you. What we call the Psalter is a collection of the various books of religious song, which grew up around and were compiled for the sake of the worship of the Second Temple, between the return under Joshua and Alexander's conquest of Palestine, say during the two centuries between 537 and 337 B.C. The First Book was compiled for the opening worship of the restored Temple by some priest connected with the early return, who draws his material exclusively from the service book of the Solomonic Temple, "The Sacred Songs of David." The Second and Third Books were prepared by Nehemiah, about a century later, and were part of his reform in the service. He not only borrows from the service books of the older Temple, but also has gathered many other poems, whose beauty of form or religious expression commended them to him as of value for sacred song. The Fourth Book was compiled by some scholar in connection with the Temple, about fifty years later, to meet a want for liturgic chorals which none of the other books supplied. Finally, toward the middle of the fourth century, the Temple board who had been charged with gathering, editing, and regulating the Sacred Books used in the service, came to take in hand the religious song of the Temple. They took the four books which were already in constant use, added to them a supplemental collection of new songs, cast the whole into a single book, giving to it as a prologue Psalm i., and as a doxology Psalm cl., and introduced it by their authority into the service of the Temple, where, with unessential variations, it ever after remained.

Christianity sprang from the womb of Judaism; the early church sang the hymns of the Temple and Synagogue, and thus it is that these old Jewish Temple songs are still sung by us.

Aside from the beauty of the Psalter in poetry and lyric song, which will commend its study as long as culture and taste and letters remain among men, it will be sung until the latest times, wherever man in his loneliness reaches out after the Eternal Being, into whose nature and relation to His creatures it penetrates deeper than any other book in the world.

Our literary study of this book and its songs is now complete. It remains to call your attention to its use in the service, and briefly explain the various liturgic notes which gradually grew up around the text, many of which are still senselessly preserved in our English version. In order to make this clear to you, I must say a word as to song and music among the Shemitic people, more especially among the Hebrews.

Song and music are twin arts, both alike the expression of the imagination through sound, as poetry through words, sculpture through form, painting through color.

Song is the expression of the imagination in sound by means of the human voice, words of course being unessential to song—a song in a foreign language, for example, may be just as perfect in its impression on us, as one the words of which we understand; music is the attempt to imitate or supplement the voice by artificial means There is no inherent relation, or necessary connection between song and music. Song is in every nation the earliest of the arts; music requires for its development at least a rude civilization.

Our present idea of song as a melodious or harmonious rhythmical expression of sound by the voice, is an occidental or modern one. Many peoples have never arrived at it; many, equal to ourselves in civilization, conceive of it quite differently. The only definition covering the ground is the one I have given. As a creation of the imagination music and song differ from mere sound quite as widely as sound does from noise.

All the books on Hebrew poetry tell us that poetry was the earliest literature, song the earliest speech of the race, and tritely refer us to the Vedas, to the songs of the Hellenic heroic epoch we call the Iliad, to the sword-song of Lamech, to the epic of the Canaanites preserved in Genesis x., further informing us that the earliest prose literature is not older than the tenth century before our era. For myself I do not believe that the primitive man in Eden lisped in numbers, or that poetry and song were developed before prose. Song has an attraction which leads the mind to revert to it, an assonance which fixes it in the memory; so, among the early peoples devoid of writing and literature, it is the song handed down from mouth to mouth that has remained while the prose has perished. Poetry and song, as products of the imagination, could not be developed before the imaginative faculty, where they had their genesis, and I doubt if the primitive man possessed this.

It is with a race as with the individual, the imagination can work as little in darkness as in the glare of noon-day. It needs the half light of twilight to give it a back-ground on which to project itself; it can work in a rude and brutish man as little as in one who has trained himself to see in nature naught but a barren sequence of fact and phenomena. The primitive man, engrossed in wringing, with scanty appliance, a bare subsistence from the soil, and in constant conflict with the forces which environed and threatened to overwhelm him, would have as little play for the imagination, as the man who has reduced the whole creation to a form of hydrogen, or ciphered it into an equation. It is in the period when passing from ignorance to knowledge, from barbarism to civilization, that the imagination of a race hitherto latent begins to work on the dim outlines which it discerns, but is not yet able to understand; it is this period in which lie the beginnings, both of the mythology and art of every people.

If we believe that the primitive Shemite was a happy shepherd or nomad, living in blissful security and pastoral innocence, careless of labor and with every want supplied by the bounty of nature, we may believe that from sheer joy of existence, in harmony with the voices of nature, he, too, sang instinctively, as the birds do.

If we believe man is a link in the development of an idea, come to the world in ignorance of the laws which govern either it or himself, compelled to win a subsistence before he can advance to knowledge, our ideas of the beginnings of song and of all the arts must be materially modified. They could not have arisen until man had subdued nature.

We have, among the Shemitic people, no traces of song until after they have come in contact with the Accadian civilization of the Euphrates valley. What their civilization was when they reached Babylonia we do not know, nor whether they had, as yet, arrived at their song-period. We do know that the oldest poetry preserved in the Genesis is of Turanian origin, and first came to the Shemites through contact with some Tatar people.

But whatever the origin of Shemitic song may be,

the Hebrews were a people who had cultivated song and who celebrated with it all their occasions of joy or sorrow. The reapers sang as they garnered the golden harvests, the vintagers as they trod out the wine press, the women as they toiled at the mill; there were love songs and marriage songs; then the keening of the mourners who went about the streets, and the dirges of the funeral train who bear their dead to the home prepared for all the living; the armies returning from victory were received by processions of singers, and often there were choruses who accompanied the troops to battle, and sang war-songs to nerve them to the charge; their banquets were accompanied by roisterings and drinking-songs which were a thorn in the side of the prophets. One of the common proverbs says, "As a signet of carbuncle set in gold, so is a concert of song at a wine banquet." At the court there were companies of paid singers, and Amos draws a graphic picture for us of the luxurious manners of the later kingdom of Israel whose effeminate nobles, reeking with perfumes, and stretched on couches of ivory, remained singing and feasting while the enemy was knocking at their very doors. Through the land there wandered minstrel troops, like the Minnesingers or Jongleurs, singing from hamlet to hamlet among the people, at their local feasts and gatherings.

There is in antiquity no people about whose song we have such clear information and yet of which we know so little. The remains of these songs which have been committed to writing belong to literature, and have in a measure been considered under lyric poetry, but the song itself, the utterance, vanished into air with the voice of the singers, and as to how they sang we can alone gather from uncertain analogy, or a tradition manufactured to the order of the want of such knowledge. In any investigation of Shemitic song the Arameans must be left out of account, their native song, just as their native literature, having irrecoverably perished.

Subsequent to the second century there sprang up, in Mesopotamian churches, a Syriac song, more perfect in form, more rich in thought, more exquisite in sentiment than any produced in the occidental churches. More than you are aware of what we now sing both in words and melody comes from Ephraem or Bardasenes or some of the Syrian hymn writers; or rather I should say, did sing until our sacred melody had been inundated by the recent outpourings of the American Polyhymnia. But Syriac church song was an exotic, growing up under Greek influence; it was surely no robbery for them to spoil the Greeks, after the Greeks had so often despoiled them. A church song thus growing up under both Christian and Greek influence, can of course not be regarded as representing native Shemitic song.

We have here, as elsewhere, to seek among the Arabs the truest expression of the Shemitic mind, the oldest type of Shemitic manners. In the song of the desert we have preserved a form of melody which approaches most nearly the song of the Hebrews. In our sense of the word it is not song, for it lacks rhythm. Rhythm is that measured rise and fall in vocal or instrumental sound, which to our ears creates its agreeable impression, corresponding to what in sculpture or architecture we call symmetry, in painting perspective. The song of the Bedouin as he drives before him his heavily laden camel, or recounts by the nightly camp fire the prowess of his tribe, is no more than what we would call recitative. In the utterance of the sound he does not propose to himself, as we do in our singing, to produce a melodious or agreeable impression. The sound is regarded merely as a vehicle for the words, and is fitted to and determined by, not only the thought, but even the very form of the words. Hence their singing is a matter of accent, of intonation and assonance, bearing no resemblance to our present song.

It is probable that both the secular and religious song of Israel were not dissimilar to this recitative song of the Bedouin, in fact from all we can gather it seems to have been the kind of song peculiar to and hereditary in the Shemitic race from the earliest times. We must first, however, glean the few scanty notices in the Psalter as to the religious song of the Temple, before we can make any statement as to its probable form.

Song being so common among the Hebrew people, David could have had no trouble in drafting the four thousand mentioned in Chronicles as connected with the Temple song. That these were all in service at any one time is improbable, the exaggerations of Josephus and the absurdities of the Talmud not deserving serious attention. There seems to have been a chosen choir of two hundred and eighty-eight singers and performers permanently attached to the Temple, by detachments of whom the daily service was sung. Drafts on the larger number were only made to furnish choruses at the feasts and on state occasions, or to fill up the ranks of the smaller and stated Temple choir. This regular choir was made up both of bass and soprano voices. How the other parts familiar to us were carried, or whether they were represented at all, we do not know. The soprano parts were carried by female singers—this once disputed question is now very clear to all scholars. Here, as so often elsewhere, the Jewish orthodoxy of modern times in allowing no female singers in the Synagogue, represents not a knowledge, but an ignorance of the past. In fact, I believe that all the restrictive religious regulations of the service and the worship, as the "Court of the Women" and many distinctions inimical to them, are the outgrowth of later times and foreign influence.

The Bedouin Shemite, on his native heath and in his pristine state, is with all his failings nature's gentleman; his courtesy and respect for woman are more delicate and refined than any produced by our modern civilization. When the Shemite came in contact with the Turk in Babylonia, he was first smudged with the touch of a race which has never appeared in history save to defile or to destroy. Among the early Shemitic people woman held a position in every way co-ordinate and equal to that of man. The regulations of the later Biblical books and of the Talmud are as little representative of primitive Shemitic or Jewish society as is the Koran. There can, at all events, be no doubt that they were in the Temple choir. We find them mentioned in the tabernacle at Shiloh, in the Solomonic Temple, and as returning both under Joshua and Ezra for the expressly stated purpose of furnishing part of the choir in the restored Temple. It is well known that under some blighting influences of a later time, what we know not, they were excluded from the choir, but it is equally clear, and proven by all the testimony it is capable of, that in the earlier time they sang in the Temple.

In regard to the inscriptions of the Psalms referring to song, I would say that they seem only to appear with those songs which were used in the worship of the First Temple. The irregular, disconnected and irrelevant way in which they are used show them to be chance choir notes.

Scholars who have carefully investigated the whole matter have reached the conclusion that, at the destruction of the Solomonic Temple, all that could be saved from the general ruin were some few songs in the sheets prepared for distribution among the choir, containing such notes as would show to what part they belonged, or suggest the key and accompaniment. Of those relating to instrumental music we will speak in a moment, but the most important of them is one of equal value for a knowledge of the song; that is the one rendered in our version, "To the chief musician," (לַמְנַצֵּחַ). Though barbarously distorted and misunderstood by the old versions, the meaning is very clear, "For the leader of the choir;" that is, it is the copy containing the score and the words used by the leader in directing the choir and orchestra. From the number of Psalms (fifty-five) which have this inscription, a German has proposed a theory that it was the leader's portfolio which was rescued.

Of the inscriptions bearing solely on song, we find, 1st, *Shir* (שִׁיר, "song," in the English version) Psalm xlvi., meaning a song to be sung without instrumental accompaniment.

2d, *Al hash-sheminith* (עַל־הַשְּׁמִינִית, English version: "upon Sheminith)," Psalms vi., xii., set for the bass voices.

3d, *Al alamoth* (עַל־עֲלָמוֹת, English version: "upon Alamoth)," set for the soprano voices, and sung as we saw a moment since by women. It does not mean tenor voices, nor are the boy choirs of the First Temple aught save a figment of some Jewish Doctor; they came in at a later day, perhaps not long prior to our era, as a substitute for women's voices. The same inscription has been preserved at the close of Psalm xlviii.

Psalm ix. has apparently been preserved on a sheet which was in use in one of the choir schools, for it has the inscription, "arranged for training of the soprano voices" (עֲלָמוֹת לַבֵּן עַל־כִּוּת לַבֵּן for עֲלָמוֹת לַבֵּן, or possibly צִלְכִוּת לַבֵּן). One might read this inscription as it stands in our English version, "upon Muth-labben," until gray without gaining from it the slightest idea.

Other of these inscriptions contain the name of some familiar melody, either sacred or secular, to whose tune the song was to be sung. You are all conversant with the similar usage in modern hymn collections. To test it I opened a celebrated hymn book and within a few pages found a hymn set to Old Hundred, and another to that bewitching Scotch ballad, "Robin Adair." Of such inscriptions there seem to be sacred melodies "Fair as lilies is thy Law" (עַל שׁוּשַׁן עֵדוּת, or אֶל־שֹׁשַׁנִּים עֵדוּת, or simply עַל־שֹׁשַׁנִּים) to which four Psalms, xlv., lx., lxix., lxxx. were sung, and "Destroy not, O God, thy people" (אַל־תַּשְׁחֵת) to which also four Psalms, lvii., lviii., lix., lxxv. were sung.

Of secular melodies you may note, "The stag at dawn" (עַל־אַיֶּלֶת הַשַּׁחַר), to which Psalm xxii. is set. It was probably a melody as familiar to them as "The stag at eve had drank his fill" is to us.

Another secular melody is, "O silent dove, what bringest thou us from out the distance" (עַל־יוֹנַת אֵלֶם רְחֹקִים), to which Psalm lvi. is set. There are many other inscriptions of a similar character, but I will not detain you by dwelling upon them.

There still remains unanswered the main question, how did they sing, but it is just the question which cannot be answered. There were no notes or written indication of the music; indeed none of the

Shemitic peoples have made use of any musical notation until within a few centuries. The melodies were preserved by tradition, and handed down orally from one generation to another, so there was constant change and liability of loss. If any of you have ever endeavored to unravel the Greek song, which had notation after a fashion, you may have some conception of the difficulties attending the study of the Jewish, which had none at all. The results of minute and technical investigations indicate that it was a recitative melody, with a few simple cadences, not unlike the song of the Arab.

To the often asked question, has any of it been preserved until our time, I would answer that there are possibly echoes of it to be found in two quarters accessible to you even here in Baltimore. 1. In the cantillation, or chanting of Scripture in the synagogue; not in the synagogue-songs, for these are all of late origin. 2. In what are known as the Gregorian melodies, which grew up in the earliest Jewish-Christian communities and were fashioned after the song they had been wont to sing in the Temple. Most scholars, whose musical training gives force to the results of their literary investigations, seem agreed that these Gregorian chants, though in many points dissimilar to the old Temple songs, are, on the whole, the truest reflex of them, which has come down to us.

THE MUSIC OF THE TEMPLE. 313

The music of the Temple might be spoken of protractedly—it need and will occupy us but a moment.

Artistically considered there is between music and song somewhat the same distinction as between lyric and epic poetry, both of which are the expression of the imagination through words, differing alone in the use of different material. So music and song are both the expression of the imagination through sound, differing alone in their use of different material—song the more subjective art, expressed through the human voice, music the more objective, by the use of some artificial substitute for it. That the origin of music, among all nations was subsequent to that of song, and that in its beginnings it was no more than an aid to the voice, will be clear to any who have studied the history of the art. The Shemitic people, according to their oldest traditions, first learned music from their contact with the Mongols; there does not seem to have been any native, or peculiar Shemitic music. Tubal, a Mongol, is represented as the father of all those who perform on instruments.

The Israelites, in their historic period, followed Egyptian musical methods and used, with slight modifications, Egyptian instruments. Were there time it would be very easy to reconstruct for you, from the paintings of the Egyptian temples and tombs, a clear picture of Egyptian music.

The Egyptians were the most cultured people of antiquity, both in the theory and practice of music. Whence their traditions of the art came, or how they arose, we do not know; like the rest of their marvellous and refined civilization, it seems to have almost dropped full grown from the clouds. One grows weary in seeing reiterated, in histories of music, the stock fables of the Greeks, as to the origin of the art, or the inventions and theories of Pythagoras and Terpander. A thousand years before Pythagoras, Egyptian music was long past its golden age; the monuments show us musical instruments as perfect, (some of them more perfect), as any which the world has since produced, while there had been developed a theory of musical art more elaborate than any known until the revolution of music by the introduction of harmony. I always relish the fine sneer of the Egyptian priest, "The Greeks! the Greeks are but children."

We must remember there was a wide difference between the music of antiquity, and what we understand by music at the present day. To appreciate it aright, you must know the distinction between melody and harmony; melody being the succession, in regular recurrence, of similar intonations or cadences; harmony, the concord arising from the union of dissonant sounds. However, we cannot delay to elaborate the distinction.

The sole office of the melodic music of antiquity was in subordination to the song, either as an accompaniment to, or interpreter of it; it was no more than a guide to the voice. This being so, we can the better understand the Hebrew Temple music, and why string-instruments, most suited for vocal accompaniment, formed, almost exclusively, the orchestra. (*Neginoth*, in the inscription of Psalm vi., means "stringed instruments.") No less than fifty-seven Psalms contain the inscription, *Midmor*, which means a song to be sung to the stringed accompaniment; then, as strings formed the chief part of the orchestra, meaning no more than "to be sung to the orchestral accompaniment."

Of stringed instruments in the Temple band, there were, 1, the *kinnor* or lyre, which was a favorite instrument of the Jews, as it was of the Greeks. It was played either with a plectrum or with the fingers. The classical writers deem the invention of its eleventh string an inspiration of genius. The Egyptians used very constantly a lyre with eighteen strings; how many the Jews used we do not know. In the ordinary band for daily service there were two lyres. 2. The *nebel*, or harp, translated in our version "Psaltery," almost precisely similar in form to our harps. It had a varying number of strings, sometimes ten (Psalm xxxiii. 2,) sometimes as many as twenty-one, and was the chief instrument in the Temple band, there being nine harps in the daily orchestra.

The only "instrument of percussion" in the Temple band was a single pair of cymbals, used by the leader in marking time, and not a direct accompaniment to the song. They were similar in form to our band cymbals. In Egypt the cymbals were never used save in connection with the worship, and the same appears to have been the usage in Israel. For popular song the tambourine, whose inventor was justly murdered by his incensed fellow-citizens, or the triangles, took the place of the cymbals. Instruments of percussion, however, even in popular music, were not employed to accompany the song; as in the present Shemitic Orient, their only use was to increase the volume of sound.

Of wind instruments there were in the band four flutes, or rather pipes, (*halil*), the only instrument besides the strings used as an accompaniment, not regularly, but to supplement the strings on certain set occasions, or in the more plaintive melodies. One of the elegiac Psalms, (Psalm v.,) contains the inscription that it was to be sung to the flutes alone.

Finally, there were two straight trumpets (*shophar*) which formed no part of the orchestra proper, but were blown for calling the people together, or indicating the different parts of the service.

The purely musical inscriptions are very obscure, both those which indicate the time of the melody (*miktam, maskil* and the like) and the sort of melody (the *gittith, shiggaion*). The most familiar of them is the much disputed *selah*, found seventy-one times in the Psalter. Scholars are for the most part now agreed, that it is no more than one of the abbreviations with which all Hebrew books are so full, standing for, סֹב לְמַעְלָה הַשָּׁר הַשִּׁיר "Let the song rise higher." If you carefully investigate its occurrence, you will find it almost without exception, in the copy from which the leader directed. It was probably only a note for guiding him in leading. Other scholars have given it a meaning not unlike "da capo" in our music, but whatever the exact shade of meaning there can not be the slightest doubt that it is merely a choir note for guiding the music. There is about as much propriety in reading it now in our service, as there would be in reading the Italian abbreviations by which the time or key of our tunes is set.

Two lyres and nine harps twanging inharmoniously; two dozen men and women chanting in unrhythmed cadence; such was the ordinary daily worship of the Solomonic Temple. On feast days it was the same, only a little more of it. We can hear at any concert what, to our taste, is better song and music than was ever heard in the Temple, from its foundation until its destruction by Titus. The world's architecture lost very little in the destruction of the Temple; quite as little has the world suffered from the loss of Hebrew music. Had the songs sung in the Temple perished, the loss to the culture and religion of men would have been irreparable. Preserved as they have been until our time, we are better able to sing and render them in music, than were the people from whose teeming and inspired imagination they sprang.

Our treatment of the Temple song and music makes no pretense of doing more than opening up the subject, and being suggestive of the manner in which it is to be approached. A single word further, and I am through.

It is a question of interest to what extent the hypophonal, or responsive singing of the people, as opposed to the antiphonal, or responsive singing of the choir, was in vogue in the Temple.

On ordinary occasions the people present seem to have had no part in the song save in the final doxologies (the *Amen* and *Hallelu-yah*). There are a few Psalms arranged for responsive singing between the choir and the people, but they were only sung on special occasions. Probably the people never did sing through the whole hymn with the choir, still less did they carry the hymn themselves as is the wont in congregational singing.

We have now reached our journey's end.

The questions connected with the translation and transmission of the Psalter to us, are not germane to the study of any one book, but are common to the entire collection of Hebrew literature, and can only justly be considered after the peculiar problems of all the separate books have been weighed and adjusted.

It has been my aim to present the Psalter to you from its literary and artistic side. I have striven to consider it in the same way that the works of Chaucer, and Shakspere, and Dante, and other masterpieces of modern poetry have been heretofore presented to you in this place.

At this late moment I can only thank you for the forbearing courtesy with which you have followed these lectures.

Their end will have been reached, if any one in my audience has been incited to a renewed reading and study of the world's deepest, tenderest and most artistic poetry, the Hebrew Psalms.

They have been the inspiration of the greatest artists and poets of our race; they will fail in their meaning for you unless they become part of your culture as well as of your faith.

www.ingramcontent.com/pod-product-compliance
Lightning Source LLC
Chambersburg PA
CBHW030741230426
43667CB00007B/796